Chinese Medicine Business Success

WHAT PEOPLE ARE SAYING

About Brigitte Linder and
Chinese Medicine Business Success

I wish I'd had this book when I first started ou t! Everything I've learned in 30 years of running a practice – and even things I never learned – can be found in this book. Highly recommended as a guide if you are beginning, a reference while you are setting up and a touchstone when you are established to check if you are being the best that you can be, business-wise.

Steven Clavey
Chinese medicine practitioner, Apricot Grove, Melbourne

As Chinese medicine practitioners, we need compassion, empathy and a pleasant bedside manner. We also need grit and determination and a good sense of humour. But above all, if we want to succeed in the highly competitive arena of private health care in Australia, we need highly refined business skills. Just a few years back there was very little out there to help people in the Australian Chinese medicine profession succeed in business. The arrival of Chinese Medicine Business Success changes all of that! This is a great book written for an Australian audience by someone who has been through the struggle and emerged victorious. It teaches the ABC's of setting up and running a Chinese medicine practice in Australia. In the short term, this book can help you pay your bills. However, if you are in this game for the long run, then this book will help you lay the foundations of your own Chinese medicine business empire. I think everyone in our profession should read it! I sure wish something like this had been around when I first graduated.

Paul McLeod
Chinese medicine practitioner, Australian Acupuncture Centre, Geelong

This book is both practical and inspiring. It is a must-read for any clinician starting out and for seasoned practitioners needing fresh ideas to enhance their clinical work and develop their business. It is a step-by-step approach to developing the values-based, ethical business foundation needed to practise your medical knowledge and to flourish in clinic. It is especially useful for those having trouble organising their internal resources to make an ethical, busy and effective clinic happen. Written by someone who has done it, this book will help you learn how to become an increasingly effective business person while continuing to love what you do.

Greg Bantick
Health & Healing Wellness Centre, Brisbane

This book is essential reading for all Chinese medicine students and graduates wanting to set up and succeed in practice. It also provides valuable ideas for existing practitioners on how to improve their Chinese medicine business. The insights reflected in Brigitte's book are a distillation of many years of experience building her business into the successful company it is while continuing to develop her excellent clinical practice skills. The foundation of her work is a love for humanity and a commitment to be a conduit of knowledge and to continue the lineage of Chinese medicine in our modern world. This is coupled with very practical strategies of how to create and build a business so that this can be actualised. I highly recommend this book to Chinese medicine students, new graduates and existing practitioners.

Dr Kylie O'Brien PhD
Adjunct Associate Professor, Torrens University, Adelaide

As a recent graduate in Chinese medicine I, like many others, face the pressure of running a business, getting desired client numbers, providing good service and meeting my clients' needs, while at the same time maintaining my authenticity within a structured framework. Brigitte's book outlines in a clear and comprehensive way the most important aspects of running a clinic and how to ensure a balance between professionalism and creative self-expression. The use of the five element framework resonated with me and has helped to motivate and inspire me for my journey ahead. The activities at the end of each chapter have allowed me to gain clarity and confidence and to refine my focus onto the most appropriate tasks. This book is practical, fun and heartfelt. Brigitte has shared her experience and provided a structure all graduates can follow to create their own unique business faster and with better results.

Vicki Iliopoulos
Chinese medicine practitioner, Venus Bay

Having been in practice since 1995, it is so pleasing to see a book dedicated to the success of the individual Chinese medicine practitioner and the industry as a whole. The learning and practice of Chinese medicine is complex enough. Add to this the trials of figuring out the intricacies of building and running a viable and successful practice and you certainly have your hands full. The beauty of this book is that it gives the perspective of highly successful and highly regarded members of the Chinese medicine industry as well as that of the author. By providing a practical framework, it also takes much of the guesswork out of being able to practice what you love and make a living doing so. By being the best we can be we have the potential to change the status quo of how health care is delivered nationally and internationally. I'm proud to recommend this resource to new graduates and veterans as an aid in making business dreams a reality and helping more people achieve the health they deserve.

Jeff Shearer
Chinese medicine practitioner, Evolve Natural Medicine, Newcastle

This is a great book. It starts with the end in mind; that is to have work wrap around life not life around work. Whether you are starting out or well established in your practice but have lost your way, this book shall restore the focus in a step-by-step manner and return you to balance through thoughtful exercises and prompts to shine the light on your own journey. Written by a practitioner with fellow acupuncturists and Chinese medicine practitioners in mind, this book is direct and pertinent to all practitioners. Be inspired.

De-Arne Campbell
Chinese medicine practitioner, To The Point
Acupuncture & Chinese Medicine, South Yarra

This book is a must-read for all Chinese medicine and other health care practitioners! Chinese Medicine Business Success is a powerful book that will enable practitioners to have a business that not only makes a difference to the community but also brings fulfilment to the practitioner. It is the first book to effectively guide practitioners to have success in both their clinical and business careers. The articulately explained methodology gives practitioners a simple and easy way for them to wake up every day filled with joy because their business has become a vehicle that works for them. They can make a big impact for their patients and also obtain freedom of time and money by having a successful business. The lessons in the book are easy to learn and apply because of the elegant framework that uses the familiar Chinese five elements as its guide. This point might well be the true genius of this book and why it will deliver such great results for those who implement it.

Dr David Dugan BDSc, Adv Dip Bus, Grad Dip
Clin Dent, Dip Fin Planning, Dip CH
Dentist/CEO Abundance Global, Brisbane

CHINESE MEDICINE BUSINESS SUCCESS

How to apply five elements for a thriving clinic

Brigitte Linder

featuring Megan Hills with *Marketing Made Easy*

Chinese Medicine Business Success: How to apply five elements for a thriving clinic

© Brigitte Linder 2019

Published by Brigitte Linder

www.brigittelinder.com

welcome@brigittelinder.com

10-12 Bluebird Court, Newhaven, VIC, 3925, Australia

Editing, design and publishing support by www.AuthorSupportServices.com

ISBN: 978-0-6480494-4-9

I dedicate this book to my grandmother Anna Linder.
She still inspires me every day.

Acknowledgements

Writing this book has taught me to be happy with where I am today. It has also made me realise that no one is perfect and that this doesn't matter as long as we are prepared to keep learning, implementing and optimising all over again.

I had a head start with a teacher who taught me everything he knew. My sincere thanks to Dr Samuel Zheng who took me under his wing and helped me transition into my practice in 2002. He was patient and gentle yet tough at times when needed. I am grateful to have met him and he remains my teacher and mentor today.

I would like to thank my colleagues in both Switzerland and Australia who have helped me out in the past 16 years and were prepared to give their time, energy and opinion to assist me with problem-solving: Jeff Shearer, Shelley Beer, Kylie O'Brien, Steven Clavey, Greg Bantick, Helen Gordon, Arnaud Versluys, Hamish Brown, Jean-Paul Staats, Peter Gigante, Lin Dong, Graham Jellett, Debra Gillick, Nadine Zaech, Simon Becker, Philipp Ehrsam and Karl Zippelius.

Sincere thanks also to Paul McLeod and Robin Marchment who provided me with invaluable feedback on the content and structure of my book.

I also express my thanks to Alex Fullerton, Wendy Millgate-Stuart and Natasha Higgins from Author Support Services. Their love for my project has been truly inspiring and their assistance and support outstanding.

I am eternally grateful to be part of the strong Tian—Zeng (Dr Tian Heming 田鶴鳴 (1883-1980)) (Zeng Rongxiu, MD 曾榮修 (1931-2012)) herbal lineage now instructed by Dr Arnaud Versluys. His in-depth knowledge, compassion, strong personality and brilliant teaching skills transformed my herbal practice and perception of herbs entirely.

Special thanks to my friend Hans Seiwald who has supported me in all my endeavours over the past 14 years. He moved to Australia with me to establish a new life. Together, we set up a herbal dispensary and clinic in regional Victoria, and he never stopped believing what I did was right, even when it was wrong. My heart, my thanks and my love go out to you. Thank you for being the caring and supportive person that you are.

To Dad, I am sorry you are missing this moment on earth, but I am sure you are watching from the heavens. Thank you for your love, your kindness and your dedication to my sister, Gabi, and me.

FOREWORD

Decades ago, to be a successful practitioner it was enough to develop and apply our knowledge and our craft and to develop trust and rapport with our patients. We studied well as undergraduates and continued our clinical and academic learning as graduates. We served our patients well on a number of levels. That was enough.

Today, we must learn how to communicate even more effectively with our patients and also with trading partners. We must devote time and energy to fulfilling many professional expectations. We need to provide appropriate information and answer a myriad of questions in an efficient but helpful way. In addition, we must fulfil our obligations for labelling, record keeping, receipting and accounting practices. So, who has time to dedicate to a marketing strategy or to care for themselves?

In *Chinese Medicine Business Success*, Brigitte constructs the scaffolding for practitioners to build a strong practice according to their individual goals and aspirations – one that is not only successful as a business model but also satisfies their personal integrity. Brigitte uses a unique and heartfelt systematic approach that covers every detail from foundation to completion and answers the many questions that all practitioners have in regard to professional obligations, the regulatory system and time management. This is all contained in a flexible framework that is evocative of our philosophical training and so rings a bell that matches our aspirations in being the clinicians we believe we should be and in supporting the kind of clinic we want to run. This is not a manual only for the newly graduated, but for those of us who need new approaches and a fresh take on how we run our business effectively whilst still being faithful to ourselves.

As just one example, the word 'marketing' brings qualms of doubt to many of us in this modern world of websites and social media. Not all of us are eager to embark on a marketing education. Yet the section 'Marketing Made Easy' is a welcome boon to those such as I who tend to recoil from such things . All resistance is demolished as the process is made clear and simple. Even a person such as myself (notoriously resistant to social media) will find it simple and clear, readable and doable. Kudos to Megan Hills for her wonderful contribution – and congratulations to Brigitte for recognising her talent.

Chinese Medicine Business Success is an impressive piece of work in its conception; it is systematic in its approach, it gives us the tools to work effectively and it is in harmony with the integrity of our practice. It is a marriage of the intellect and the heart, resonating with our clinician's heart as well as our business manager's mind.

Innovative in its concept and practical in its application, this book is congruent with the ethics and philosophy of Chinese medicine which, in itself, is structured and logical, while simultaneously offering flexibility. I just wish I had had this remarkable resource at my fingertips two decades ago.

Robin Marchment
BA (Hons), BHSc (Acup), Adv Dip HSc (Acup)
Cert Gyn (China), Dip Lang (Chin), Adv Dip HSc (TCM)
Registered Herbalist and Acupuncturist

PREFACE

I wake early in the morning because my brain works the best at that time. It hasn't always been like this but since running a business many of my habits have changed. Each morning, I take my dog, Pippa, for a walk on the beach. To me, that's the best way to start the day. It's when the Yin transitions to Yang. The world in and around me awakes, the energy is unspoiled and thoughts are the clearest. The two of us often witness the sun coming up across the water in the East. If it's a calm day, flocks of birds are busy setting themselves up for the new day.

I love this time of day with its fresh air and new qi as it allows me to arrange my thoughts and cherish my plans. Often, especially if I have challenges in my clinic or I have to sort something out, these morning outings give me the time and space to come to a good solution that feels right.

Building a business can cause anxiety and stress at various levels. Thankfully, I can share those fears with a team in my business, Safflower Chinese Medicine Dispensary & Clinic, as we tend to work things out better together. I also tell myself that Rome wasn't built in a day and that everything good truly takes time. Within this perpetually evolving process, I take great care that my values and goals are reflected in all my actions.

I have never been very artistic. I don't paint or make sculptures or other handy items, but I express my creativity in my business. My business reflects who I am. The profession that I intuitively chose, being a Chinese medicine practitioner, ultimately allows me to express myself as me. I truly feel that I have embraced my inner power or essence, which I call my 'inner emperor'.

Now, don't think I knew all this from the beginning. In fact, I remember when starting out that I was incredibly nervous with patients and unsure of my treatments, not knowing when and how to follow up. Managing patients was difficult for me as I am originally from Switzerland and things are different in Australia. It takes so much time to look after the administration required to run a clinic, let alone the need for marketing and finding new patients to fill up empty spaces in an appointment book. Witnessing how some new graduates struggle when first starting out, just as I did, encouraged me to write this book.

When I first migrated to regional Victoria, I felt totally isolated. Now, after a decade in Australia, I feel strongly connected to the Chinese medicine industry and to my purpose. I hope that this book will assist many other practitioners to achieve the same.

As new graduates, it is essential to have access to experienced practitioners. Expertise comes with years of practice and separation from the main body of the profession can be tough. We forget that only a few steps separate us, much like the concept of 'six degrees of separation' whereby everyone in the world is only six or fewer steps away from each other. I find this an amazing notion and feel in reality that it often pans out exactly like this. In fact, often there are less than six steps involved. All we have to do is take one step towards each other and I encourage new graduates to do that more often. Never feel disheartened if your attempts to connect with a more experienced practitioner fail as you will eventually find someone who is prepared to step towards you too.

This book is an accumulation of my knowledge, expertise and practical skills in running a Chinese medicine practice. During my 17 years in the Chinese medicine industry, I have undertaken various courses and ongoing training in many areas from acupuncture and herbs to Canonical herbal training. I have studied channels and convergences and five element acupuncture. I have attended various seminars and workshops on how to run a successful business and taken advice from people who already run a successful practice.

With this book, I hope I can honour everyone who has been part of my learning journey and assisted me to be where I am today.

This book describes a simple and easy-to-apply generic system that anyone can use. I believe it also allows for a great range of self-expression and individuality in conducting business in the Chinese medicine industry. It is my hope that it will help both new and established practitioners to implement a framework that works well for them so their years of study and training can bear fruit in a successful practice with happy patients and a happy practitioner.

This book is also about YOU. It is a gentle reminder to apply the five elements in your life and embrace the fact that our universe truly is an exchange of Yin and Yang. My reflective walks on the beach take me back to myself and the nourishing of self: to reflect, to think and to be mindful. Self-care is incredibly important in my life and helps me to remain focused and available for my patients. The rhythms of life and our perception changes daily, just as the tide comes in and leaves the shore once more. And just as the waves and wind change the landscape, self-care has the ability to transform the body and mind.

Our profession with its incredibly rich traditions offers so much in the way of treatment and therapy. Let us embrace it fully and apply it to our lives, our practice and to ourselves. I have great hopes that Chinese medicine practitioners in Australia will indeed succeed in establishing a strong profession with a framework of maintaining and regaining health that surpasses all expectations.

I welcome feedback and stories so that we can learn from each other and contribute to our industry. Please connect with me via email at welcome@brigittelinder.com.

CONTENTS

ELEMENT 4: SYSTEMS

ELEMENT 5: REVIEW

APPENDICES

INTRODUCTION

Chinese medicine practitioners represent less than 1% of the workforce in Australia. Even though there is a growing demand for Chinese medicine modalities such as acupuncture and Chinese herbal medicine, practitioners in Australia are struggling to operate profitable clinics. On average, an acupuncturist earns an average salary of $53,257 per year, compared with the average salary for a chiropractor or an osteopath of $70,423 per year.[1] I have written this book with the aim of raising the figure reflected in this dismaying statistic.

Chinese Medicine Business Success: How to apply five elements for a thriving clinic encompasses all facets of establishing a successful practice and a thriving business. This book demonstrates an incredible amount of dedication to the Chinese medicine industry. It is the first book of its kind in Australia and has been written primarily for Chinese medicine practitioner graduates looking for guidance in transitioning into their own business. This book will hopefully also inspire more experienced practitioners to look at the way they practise in a different light and provide them with some new ideas.

As practitioners of Chinese medicine, we are familiar with the five elements or five phases of existence. It is a comprehensive system based on natural phenomena that determine five master groups or patterns. In the clinical setting we use it to explain how conditions are interconnected and how they impact on various systems of the body. Inspired by this, I have created a practical, easy-to-follow framework called the '5 Element Chinese Medicine Practice Success Model' to help you achieve success in your clinical practice. This model contains five simple elements which are presented in five chapters in this book. Each Element is important for long-term business success. All have been tested in my practice and are entirely transferable.

Over the past decade, this framework has assisted me in establishing meaningful connections, not only within the Australian Chinese medicine profession but also with my patients. It has kept me and my business, Safflower Chinese Medicine Dispensary & Clinic, running at optimal levels. It has allowed me to grow and develop both as a practitioner and as an individual. I still use this framework today both professionally and personally.

One key aspect within my 5 Elements Model is marketing, especially marketing that is smart and doesn't cost an arm and a leg. Marketing has been crucial to my own business. I graduated from my undergraduate course in Melbourne in 2001, moved back to Switzerland in 2002 and practised in my homeland for six years. At the same time, I started working for a Swiss dispensary service and after a few years moved on to become a consultant. In this role, I combined my experience as a practitioner and my expertise in herbal dispensing with leadership and team integration.

Upon returning to Australia and setting up practice in 2008, I received valuable assistance in implementing marketing activities from Megan Hills, Health Practice Business Coach at Ethical Practice. I am thrilled that Megan has agreed to present her gems of marketing wisdom in this book. Megan's key areas of expertise are marketing and business training, creative and cultural enterprise mentorship, design and illustration, and arts administration. She not only has the 'eye' and the 'words' but brings in that creative ingredient that is often required for effective and low-cost marketing. She presents detailed information and exact instructions on how you might improve the identity and visibility of your clinic and business as a whole.

You will also hear firsthand from well-known and valued colleagues who are doing well in the industry in Australia. I am honoured that they are prepared to share their secrets, their successes and the challenges they have faced throughout their business journey. Towards the end of the book, you will find useful information on suppliers, professional associations, training course providers, business mentors as well as recommended further reading.

This book is formatted so you can quickly look something up or dive into chapters more deeply. Each Element chapter concludes with a few thoughts on 'Elemental Self-Care' to help guide you towards some self-care followed by a range of activities. These activities are designed to help you plan and run your business confidently by integrating the knowledge shared in a step-by-step manner. It's important to action the activities and take notes or record your answers on your favourite device. For the information to come alive, it's best to go through the activities as you finish reading each Element, however they can be done after reading the entire book. Downloadable templates are available on my website to help you keep track of the process.

Setting up and running a practice is a step-by-step process. I encourage you to embrace the process fully. This book is not an academic piece; rather, it reflects my personal approach to building, running and managing a practice, and making a good living from it. I do not suggest that this book provides all the answers but it will provide new graduates with guidance on how to transition into a successful practice. The more easily and effectively new practitioners can integrate into our remarkable profession, the stronger the foundation will be to enable their business and the industry as a whole to flourish.

> Setting up and running a practice is a step-by-step process.

As part of a new generation of practitioners, you have incredible potential to change the face of our industry, to bring about new energy, to work differently and to embrace the idea that we can achieve much more as a team and help our profession to mature. If you truly crave recognition and wide-ranging acceptance for Chinese medicine practice – and believe me, if you don't yet, you soon will – your confidence and professionalism will strengthen solidarity within the industry and bring maturity to the ranks.

As a strong profession, we can help more people. As a strong practitioner, you can help more people and create a successful income and business at the same time. It's really that simple.

SNAPSHOT OF THE 5 ELEMENT CHINESE MEDICINE PRACTICE SUCCESS MODEL

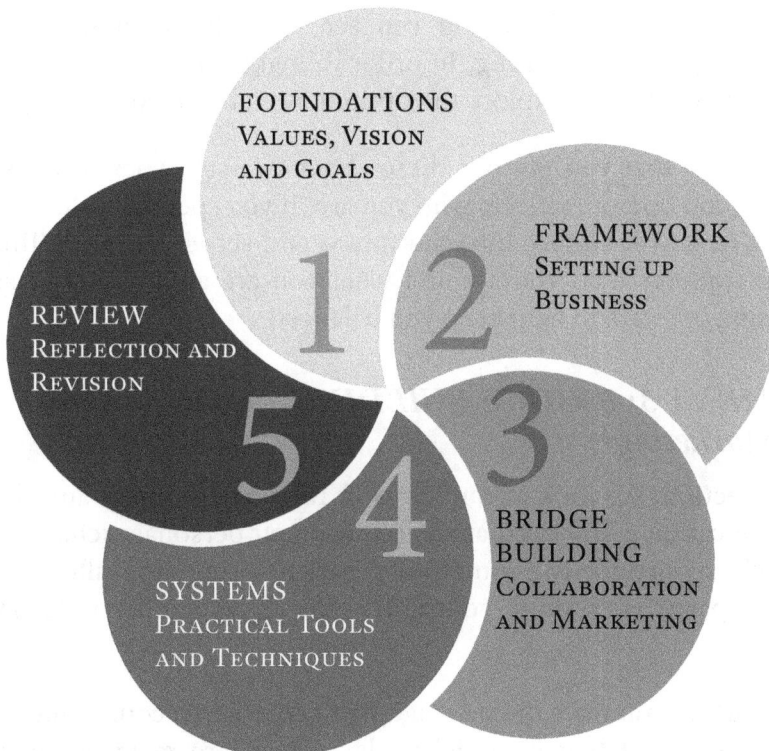

FOUNDATIONS
VALUES, VISION
AND GOALS

1

FRAMEWORK
SETTING UP
BUSINESS

2

REVIEW
REFLECTION AND
REVISION

5

3

4

BRIDGE
BUILDING
COLLABORATION
AND MARKETING

SYSTEMS
PRACTICAL TOOLS
AND TECHNIQUES

ELEMENT 1: FOUNDATIONS – Values, Vision and Goals

Behind the power and force of everything is the initial spark. Within that spark is the entire solution – the pathway and the ultimate achievement. Visions are powerful because they are intrinsic to our own existence. This first Element and first part of the framework will assist you in tapping into your own vision.

Your vision combined with your values will help you to set your goals. Values can change over time, but they are always guiding forces that direct our actions and decisions on a daily basis. To align your goal setting with your vision and values is not difficult, but it requires some reflection and planning.

ELEMENT 2: FRAMEWORK – Setting up Business

Once your vision is crystallised, the focus is on you. This Element covers the basics of how you can set yourself up in business immediately after graduating. In order to make good decisions for the future you need to explore the options available to you.

The message that you put out there about yourself, your business and how you operate reflects who you are. If you spend a little time refining it, it will endure into the future and serve you well. This section explores who you are and what you are about, as well as discussing self-care to help keep you balanced.

ELEMENT 3: BRIDGE BUILDING – Collaboration and Marketing

In this section, we look at ourselves in relation to others and the communication pathways that we follow in our personal exchanges. 'Others' may include the community, patients, suppliers, alliances, business partners, alumni, colleagues, friends and other industry partners.

This Element examines the message that you wish to communicate in order to build that essential bridge. There are many ways to promote your message and it is essential that you have great clarity on exactly how to do so. Megan Hills, Ethical Practice Business Coach, addresses this issue in the marketing section in a practical, easy-to-follow manner.

ELEMENT 4: SYSTEMS – *Practical Tools and Techniques*

Structure and organisation are essential for continued success. This Element encourages you to put systems in place to make your life easier – not only as a practitioner but also as a business owner.

This Element outlines systems to support you on a daily, quarterly and annual basis. It is also an essential prerequisite for Element 5 because reflection is more easily applied to all areas once a system is in place as it will then become apparent what works and what needs restructuring or modifying.

ELEMENT 5: REVIEW – *Reflection and Revision*

Reflection allows us to develop, deepen and strengthen. Reflection also provides room for change. In this Element, several established practitioners share their experience, challenges and successes.

By combining reflection and revision with real-life experience as a practitioner, you will grow and develop, and become more confident and knowledgeable about your clinical practice as well as about yourself as a person. Regular review throughout your career will nurture positive change in your clinical setting, in yourself and potentially also in the message that you impart as you journey towards business success.

ELEMENT 1: FOUNDATIONS

Values, Vision and Goals

"Your vision will become clear only when you look into your heart. Who looks outside, dreams. Who looks inside, awakens."

—Carl Jung

To create a successful Chinese medicine practice, you have to set goals and plan your success. Success is a word that means different things to different people: it can include financial reward, helping as many people as possible, becoming a confident and well-respected practitioner, building a beautiful clinic or finding the answers to complex questions. Success is very individual. Your anticipated vision of success must be aligned with your goals and you need a clear plan.

Before you dive into planning your vision and goals, however, it is essential to know your core values. These are your drivers in life, part of your personality even, and will be at the core of your bigger vision or 'why'. Without knowing your values, you may set goals that set you on a path to somewhere that is not in alignment with *who* you are and therefore your 'success' won't sit right.

KNOW YOUR VALUES

As a Chinese medicine practitioner, you have the potential to flavour your business with your own style and to bring your own personality into the treatment room and into your interaction with patients. Intrinsic to this are your values.

Personal values are the general expression of what is most important to you. They influence your thoughts, words and actions on a daily basis. They also assist you in growing and developing towards a specific purpose, hence their importance in defining your vision and goals. It's essential to think about your vision and tap into the bigger picture to find your 'why' of what you do and the values that come with it.

Some practitioners may say they simply wish to help people to have better health or regain health. Some may say it's more about assisting clients in the clinic space in a particular way that is flavoured with their own personal style. You might feel comfortable talking to patients about their emotional state and tackle their path to healing from a psychological point of view. Conversely, focusing on bodywork might be easier for you and so you concentrate more on integrating aspects that fit in with that approach such as massage, acupressure and acupuncture.

Your values might not be crystal clear to you when you start thinking about them. The fact that there are so many possible values to narrow down to which is the best fit for you at this stage of your life doesn't make it any easier.

The values I have chosen originate in my past as well as being qualities that I look for in others nowadays. The reason for choosing them is based on the way I was brought up, the negative experiences in my life (which taught me a lot about myself) and the expectations others had of me. They also originate from my religious orientation and what I felt other people in my life were lacking. My values might have changed slightly over the years and could still change in the future, but for now, I have narrowed them down to four: accountability, honesty, expressiveness and justice.

Identifying your own values will help you make better decisions for yourself and your business. For instance, you will choose suppliers who share similar values to you and this will make your collaborations a lot easier.

Some examples of values are found in the following list.[2] You will refer to these when you investigate your values in the activities at the end of this chapter.

Accountability	Determination	Hard work
Accuracy	Devoutness	Health
Achievement	Diligence	Helping society
Adventurousness	Discipline	Holiness
Altruism	Discretion	Honesty
Ambition	Diversity	Honour
Assertiveness	Dynamism	Humility
Balance	Economy	Independence
Being the best	Effectiveness	Ingenuity
Belonging	Efficiency	Inner harmony
Boldness	Elegance	Inquisitiveness
Calmness	Empathy	Insightfulness
Carefulness	Enjoyment	Intelligence
Challenge	Enthusiasm	Intellectual status
Cheerfulness	Equality	Intuition
Clear-mindedness	Excellence	Joy
Commitment	Excitement	Justice
Community	Expertise	Leadership
Compassion	Exploration	Legacy
Competitiveness	Expressiveness	Love
Consistency	Fairness	Loyalty
Contentment	Faith	Making a difference
Continuous	Family-oriented	Mastery
improvement	Fidelity	Merit
Contribution	Fitness	Obedience
Control	Fluency	Openness
Cooperation	Focus	Order
Correctness	Freedom	Originality
Courtesy	Fun	Patriotism
Creativity	Generosity	Perfection
Curiosity	Goodness	Piety
Decisiveness	Grace	Positivity
Democracy	Growth	Practicality
Dependability	Happiness	Preparedness

Professionalism	Service	Thoroughness
Prudence	Shrewdness	Thoughtfulness
Quality-oriented	Simplicity	Timeliness
Reliability	Soundness	Tolerance
Resourcefulness	Speed	Traditionalism
Restraint	Spontaneity	Trustworthiness
Results-oriented	Stability	Truthfulness
Rigour	Strategic thinking	Understanding
Security	Strength	Uniqueness
Self-actualisation	Structure	Unity
Self-control	Success	Usefulness
Selflessness	Support	Vision
Self-reliance	Teamwork	Vitality
Sensitivity	Temperance	
Serenity	Thankfulness	

CREATE YOUR VISION

Once you have spent a bit of time assessing these values and the reasons for choosing those most important to you, you then need to create a vision. In fact, a vision is intrinsic to your very own existence. Your vision, based on your values, will naturally generate your goals and your plan to achieve that vision. It's time well invested for a bright future, as hard as it may seem right now to engage with the process.

In my experience, your vision and plans should be set for the next 10 years, broken into 12month and 3year steps. A plan is not only critical to help you achieve your vision but is also essential for an enjoyable experience. You may find it a difficult task to determine exactly where you want to be in 12 months, 3 years or 10 years simply because you don't know or are unsure about your journey. Well, now is a good time to spend some energy on it.

Any decision you make now should be in line with what you want to achieve in the long term.

Although it is difficult to start planning when you have little practical knowledge to base decisions on, your clinical practice and business journey must be mapped out; this is non-negotiable. If you visit another country, you don't just walk or drive there. There are oceans to cross, mountains to climb and rivers to pass. There are seasonal influences, foreign currencies, political circumstances and cultural differences to take into consideration. From a business perspective, it is important that you have some idea about what direction you would like to take as most decisions you take now will greatly affect your future. Therefore, any decision you make now should be in line with what you want to achieve in the long term.

A decade passes very quickly. In that time, I would love to see humanity taking big steps towards acknowledging that we are all made of the same material, that we have a similar goal of happiness and that we can support each other best by helping one another. My values of accountability, honesty, expressiveness and justice will guide me towards achieving this. How so? They will assist me in making decisions to establish programs, involve other individuals, choose locations that are conducive to the cause, raise money with and from certain organisations, and much more.

My 'grand' vision, which extends beyond current circumstances, is to create a global mentorship program. I associate the ten year mark with achieving my grand vision.

> I associate the ten year mark with achieving my grand vision.

I highly recommend that you take the time now to think about the future and where you would like to see yourself. Now is the crucial time to give space and thought to your short- and long-term future to ensure you make something out of the time and resources you invested in your studies.

Your degree in Chinese medicine offers a great opportunity for your own vision. You might want to be involved in the first Chinese medicine hospital in the Southern Hemisphere or the first cancer centre treating patients with Eastern modalities only. If your values are strong, your vision will be too.

Values create visions by simply extending the qualities of those values into what you have been dreaming about – something that you would love to do or have always wanted to be involved in.

Setting goals

Once you have explored your vision and plan for the future, the next step is to think about some goals – milestones and markers – to help you to stay on track towards the achievement of your vision. These goals are not just the numbers in your plan, but they also include an attribute or a quality. A qualitative milestone could be being confident in treating a certain condition or working with a particular (difficult) patient or an age group such as children or seniors. It could simply mean that you feel ready to talk to banks or investors about your hospital project.

Knowing your goals will assist you in setting priorities. The more succinctly your goals are expressed, the clearer and more attainable they become. Below are some questions to reflect on or discuss with a trusted friend, partner or colleague to help you achieve clarity on your goals. The activities at the end of the chapter also provide an opportunity to finetune your goals and write them down.

In his book *Goals! How to Get Everything You Want – Faster Than You Ever Thought Possible*, Brian Tracy says that writing your goals down is essential.[3] Tracy discusses a Harvard University study that took place between 1979 and 1989 in which graduates of an MBA were asked if they had clearly written goals for their future and plans to accomplish them. Only 3% of students had written goals and plans. 13% had goals but not in writing and 84% had no specific goals at all. After ten years, the same graduates were interviewed with the following results: The 13% who had goals but not in writing were earning on average twice as much as the 84% who had no goals at all. The 3% who had written goals were earning on average ten times as much as the other 97% of graduates combined.

Proven results such as these confirm that having clarity of your goals and writing them down magnifies your chance of success significantly.

Consider the following:

- What things in life do I cherish the most?
- What areas of my life do I love? Why is that so?
- How do I want to feel around others?
- What got me here?
- Why did I do what I did in the past?
- How do others treat me?
- What do my friends see in me and what do they love about me?
- What do my patients say about me?
- How do I view my clinic/business?
- Do I want to practise in a particular field, a particular location or a particular style?
- What income do I hope to make?
- Is it important for me to work with others or would I prefer to be a sole operator?
- What am I going to focus on in my business?

By giving this process space and a reasonable amount of time and focus, yet without being too pedantic, you will get closer to your essence, the power, the engine that drives, that inner flame – your emperor. You will be able to create single sentences about yourself that resonate with you strongly and truly reflect who you are. Striving to determine a life purpose is a key moment in anyone's life. I can assure you that devoting time and effort in this area is well invested and will make your life much easier.

Below are examples of some of my goals that help me move towards my vision. As you will notice, I have set qualitative and quantitative goals. Additionally, I have listed both my personal and professional goals as they go hand in hand. I started with my long-term goal... my grand vision. After that, I narrowed it down to the next 3 years and then the 12 months immediately ahead. When setting your goals, and especially the 3year goals, it is important to ensure they truly reflect what you want to do and achieve.

	Personal goals	Professional goals
10 years **Vision**	Spend two months per year exploring places I have never been Link my travels with community work Be financially independent	Reduce my workload to two days per week in clinic Mentor 30 graduates per year Design a global mentorship program
3 years **Milestone**	Work in Nepal for one month Go on a three-week retreat in Nepal Increase financial buffer to $20,000 Pay off all debts Offer eight hours of community work per month	Be proficient in using Shang Han Lun and Jin Gui Yao Lue formulas Use Dr Tan's methods Obtain good results in 90% of my patients Present a paper on the impact of mentorship programs in our industry
12 months **Goals to get the ball rolling**	Have four weeks of holidays per year Spend two hours per week with my friends Go camping four weekends of the year Offer two hours of community work per month Read 12 books per year Build a financial buffer of $5,000 Have at least 12 acupuncture treatments myself over the year	Treat 30 patients per week and generate $2,400 per week Learn Dr Tan's balancing method Memorise top 50 Shang Han Lun formulas Offer three educational events on various topics to the community Connect with at least ten other health practitioners and learn what they do Promote services to local government

Techniques to map your path

As you start brainstorming your values, vision and goals, particularly in the activities at the end of this chapter, you might find mind mapping techniques quite useful to map your path. There are great advantages to using mind mapping rather than conservative note taking. Mind mapping is a graphical and very visual way to represent ideas and concepts. It's a tool that assists in structuring information to create a map of what's in your mind. You don't need a computer and mind mapping software to have a go; simply use a piece of paper and some pens and start scribbling away.

Consolidating your goals

Once you have set your goals, constantly remind yourself of them – you can read them, listen to them or look at a picture of them every day. As your mental plane absorbs your goals, your brain receives the message and helps you with every small step towards achieving them. Your goals now drive every single action in you and create alignment between you and your purpose.

Should you choose to play it by ear or let things happen organically, the chances are that achieving your goals won't just happen unless you are fortunate to be in the right place at the right time with the right idea and the right people. Our brains are made for procrastination and the sidetracking that occurs might not get you very far.

Test this theory on a goal to free write 1,000 words every day (something I did when writing this book). Without planning how to achieve this goal, you will find that you get up from your desk for another glass of water and on the way to the kitchen you will come across your unopened mail, so you will attend to that. Then you remember you had done a load of washing and now need to hang that out. Then once in the garden, you will notice the weeds are crying out to you. You will see the neighbour you haven't seen for a couple of weeks and start chatting. Then the phone rings. Then you need to check emails. In the end, you will find you have only written

> For planning to be effective, it is essential to follow your vision.

50 words and the day is over. This is not how you achieve anything... well, not very quickly anyway.

For planning to be effective, it is essential to follow your vision. It sounds such simple advice, but we are so busy running our day-to-day lives that our plan is relegated to second place unless we consciously keep it at the front of our mind. Otherwise, five years will pass in a flash and you will find yourself asking where you are going.

As your profession is a part of your life, be sure to include your personal vision and goals. It is part of you. Everything starts with you and it is you who must drive it to go where you want it to go. It is in your control. The time is now as you are about to embark on your new endeavour as a Chinese medicine practitioner. With more life experience you now know yourself a little better. Know where you want to go so you can start walking that path confidently with clarity and purpose. You can now plan your actions and your list of things to do. Element 4 discusses tools that can help you along the way.

In this chapter, I have encouraged you to think about your vision and goals for both your professional and private life. It's easy to skip through this section and think that you don't want or need to do this. But believe me, everything is in the planning. So please, if you are at the beginning of your business venture and you are serious about it, do it now! You can start with the activities that follow. Do the best you possibly can with the activities. Know how important it is for you to set yourself up for the future and to become a successful practitioner aligned with your purpose. Our profession also needs you to be assertively set on the future in order to assist future generations in this process of transition. The only way to know where you are going is to set goals.

ELEMENTAL SELF-CARE

As Chinese medicine practitioners we know that with flow comes ups and downs. We are also aware that each of the five elements has a quality. In this first Element on values, vision and goals, we embrace the wood energy – the planning. Sitting down and planning doesn't come easily to a lot of practitioners as we just want to help people feel better. Therefore, there is a tendency to burn out quickly. A little planning supported by the wood energy – the season of spring and growth – helps avoid that.

Please take your time to plan ahead as much as possible. You could set a date in, say, November for a strategic planning day (either on your own or with other practitioners) to plan the whole year ahead. I always plan my clinic breaks and all of my activities ahead of time. Planning helps me to feel more relaxed. Although planning requires time and effort, I assure you it is time well spent.

☑ ELEMENT 1 ACTIVITIES

These foundational activities are exceptionally important for the bright future of a practitioner. Please make sure you spend ample time and put all your sincerity and heart into them as these activities will assist you greatly in setting the foundations for a solid and sustainable future. You will find mind mapping and rich picture techniques useful to apply here.

1.1: Identify your top three values

This first activity will have you reflecting on your values and your 'why' as a foundation for creating your grand vision.

1. Take a look at the values table on page 11 and choose ten values that resonate with you.
2. Go through your list of ten values and cross five out.
3. Now choose your top three values from the remaining five on the list. Why are those top three values so important for you? Use the values that you have chosen for yourself as guidance in setting your vision and goals in the next activities.

1.2: Explore your 'grand' vision

This exercise will provide you with clarity about your vision. It will help to focus on your future and set the right goals and plans to get there. For example, if the outcome that you want to become proficient in (ie. your vision) is working with mental health conditions, you are most likely not going to choose to work in a clinic that focuses on autoimmune conditions.

Most people don't dare to dream big enough. This is your moment to encounter your big vision. Dare to be different, no matter how scary this might feel. It's a moment to bring your essence into your life as a practitioner. While doing this exercise, it is important that you do not think about *how* you will achieve your vision, but simply come up with the vision itself.

4. Sit down with a trusted friend, partner or mentor and start exploring your vision for your practice by talking about it and naming goals and aspirations. Is your dream to own and run a multidisciplinary clinic or is your dream to work with a certain age group? What difference do you want to make in people's lives? Do you have a calling to work with minorities? Is your biggest goal to work overseas? Is your aim to practise a certain modality proficiently? What is your personal dream? Dare to express it!

5. As you consider ideas, notice your feelings and any revelations, images or thoughts that accompany them. Feelings might be accompanied by sensations in your body: a tingling sensation, butterflies in your stomach, a warm feeling in your chest, a buzzing feeling at the back of your head, a general emotion of feeling happy and content, or a moment of truth – the feeling that everything aligns in time and space.

6. Write your findings down or record them on your favourite device.

1.3: Define your 10-year goals

You have now spent some time thinking about your vision. The next step is to set your goals. Importantly, you need to start with your long-term goal – your grand vision.

7. Sit down and think about your long-term goals. What are you setting out to achieve in the next ten years? Be as clear as possible. Make them big and prosperous; do not hold back.

8. Write these goals down or record them on your favourite device.

Once you are happy with these goals and they fully resonate with you at this point in your life, take the next step and narrow them down to the next 3 years, then the 12 months immediately ahead of you.

1.4: Determine your 3-year goals

9. Sit down and think about what you want to achieve in 3 years' time? Be as clear as possible. Make these goals a milestone between now and your 10year plan. Make sure that some of the goals are challenging but still truly reflect what you want to do. You might plan to buy a clinic, double your income, educate yourself further in a particular area of interest or go overseas to work for a not-for-profit organisation for 12 months.

10. Write these goals down or record them on your favourite device.

1.5: Set your 12-month goals

11. Sit down and think about what you want to achieve in the next 12 months. Remember the bigger picture – your 10year grand vision. Be as clear and concise as possible and make these goals a milestone between now and your 3year goals.

12. Write these goals down or record them on your favourite device.

Congratulations, you have completed the most important part of your journey. For further worksheets and templates, go to www.brigittelinder.com.

ELEMENT 2: FRAMEWORK

SETTING UP BUSINESS

"Knowing others is wisdom; Knowing the self is enlightenment.
Mastering others requires force; Mastering
the self requires strength."

—Lao Tzu

During your studies over the past few years, you have learnt incredible new skills, theories and techniques. You have discovered new concepts, laws and regulations. You have connected with new people who have become close friends, colleagues and mentors. Now, a new phase of your life is starting and it is time to put your skills into practice.

This Element takes a closer look at you, your responsibilities and how you can best determine how and where to work. There are many choices in this industry and you want to make the best one for yourself. Give yourself ample time to find your rhythm in your practice. To start, as discussed in Element 1, make sure you know the direction you are heading. Give yourself plenty of opportunities to determine that direction, as it will make such a tremendous difference to how you approach things. By having a strong vision, you will set yourself up on a clearly defined path and it will provide you with purpose and drive.

You will need to consider how you can integrate evidence-based medicine with your practice of Chinese medicine. Take some time to think about how the West can live symbiotically with the East and how your modality can be an attractive offer to prospective patients.

As a registered professional, you have basic responsibilities and these are covered with the help of the Chinese Medicine Board of Australia. There are many advantages to membership of a professional association, but it can be hard to decide which one to join. To help you make that decision, I have compiled a list of the most popular ones together with their ethos and areas of focus.

Current trends in treatment methods in Australia are also investigated as well as the importance of finding your authentic style in practising. Flowing on from that, we look at some different practice structures. Depending on your vision, your goals and your preferred style, you need to decide whether to work for yourself, as a team member or as an independent contractor. If you are currently a student, I recommend that you explore your values and goals, the different styles of practice available and the way you envisage working during your last 12 months at university as this will help you get started more effectively once you enter the profession.

This section concludes with the importance of staying connected to self (and others) and developing a self-care plan which is essential for your happiness, the happiness of your clients and, ultimately, your business success.

EVIDENCE-BASED MEDICINE AND CHINESE MEDICINE

Although evidence-based medicine (EBM) is part of your tertiary study, it can seem an estranged concept to traditional Chinese medicine practice. The evidence-based Western-style approach to medicine does not reflect the clinical reality of Chinese medicine. Chinese medicine was traditionally taught in an apprentice-based setting, whereas modern-day training takes place in an academic setting. The traditional transference of knowledge, skills and insight has been phased out and replaced with a Western educational approach. It's probable that we have lost a little of our true identity as Chinese medicine practitioners in the process. By true identity, I mean that Chinese medicine in its original form is a system of empirical and practical knowledge of complex parts that work as a functional whole to treat the whole person rather than a single symptom.

So, how does EBM work for Chinese medicine practitioners? What is EBM anyway? The purpose of EBM is to help health professionals make better decisions regarding treatment. It prides itself on up-to-date and scientifically proven information on the various medical options that are available. Although the range of EBM is limited, we can't ignore its existence or power as patients seek evidence-based treatments for their conditions. For a start, it's great to use EBM to attract patients and catch their attention.

A recent review published by the Australian Acupuncture and Chinese Medicine Association (AACMA) called *The Acupuncture Evidence Project: A Comparative Literature Review* followed the EBM model and concluded that acupuncture has a positive effect in the following eight conditions[4]:

1. Migraine prophylaxis

2. Headache

3. Chronic low back pain

4. Allergic rhinitis

5. Knee osteoarthritis

6. Chemotherapy-induced nausea and vomiting

7. Post-operative nausea and vomiting

8. Post-operative pain.

This systematic review further concluded that acupuncture has a potential positive effect on an additional 38 conditions and suggested that more research is necessary to determine the effectiveness of acupuncture on a further 70 conditions currently showing unclear/insufficient evidence and 5 conditions showing little or no evidence.

With its connection to evidence-based medicine, this type of valuable information assists the Chinese medicine modality of acupuncture to be brought into the Western medical setting. It does not, however, provide a complete answer for a Chinese medicine practitioner. When I practise, I keep both systems separate in my mind and in my explanation to patients. I mention to my patients the benefits of evidence-based studies but also make it very clear to them that every individual is different and as a Chinese medicine practitioner I treat every person as a unique, distinctive being. In my opinion, this is the best way to utilise both systems.

My approach is to use EBM to my own advantage. For example, in order to attract new patients, I would use this research and make a big deal out of these eight conditions in my communications (ie. advertorials, website, eNews). At the same time, I would explain the limitations of the research for other conditions and, most importantly, emphasise that Chinese medicine takes into account that everyone is different so patients understand that EBM has its limitations and other avenues are worth exploring.

Chinese medicine assessment and diagnosis is very detailed. It encompasses the person's constitution, the identification of harmful factors (internal and external), the history of the illness, and the patient's personal history, diet and lifestyle. From that, a concise treatment plan is developed to address the disharmony and a series of activities (diet, lifestyle and exercise) implemented to reduce the possibility of further occurrence.

Chinese medicine is a brilliant system but it is limiting if you try to compare or align it with the approach of Western medicine. Although certain protocols work well, using them as a basic approach while considering the patient's constitution works best in my experience. This includes protocols such as the National Acupuncture Detoxification Association (NADA) protocol for addictions, mental health issues, and disaster and emotional trauma[5], and the acupuncture protocol for pre- and post-transfers in IVF treatments[6].

The same applies to prescribing Chinese herbal formulas. Research has shown that certain herbs contain compounds that have an effect on a condition. Take, for example, curcumin, the most active constituent of turmeric. Cancer Research UK states: "A few laboratory studies on cancer cells have shown that curcumin has anti cancer effects. It seems to be able to kill cancer cells and prevent more from growing. It has the best effects on breast cancer, bowel cancer, stomach cancer and skin cancer cells... "[7] Chinese herbal medicine actually uses three different species of turmeric: Jiang Huang (Curcuma Longa), E Zhu (Curcuma Zedoaria) and Yu Jin (Curcuma Aromatica). Each of these herbs has different qualities and they work best when combined with other substances in a formula that addresses a disharmony pattern. The utilisation of all three species through the holistic approach of Chinese medicine for a variety of pathological patterns is surely an advantage over the use of isolated compounds which is likely the approach taken in EBM.

Explaining the difference to patients

Every day I explain to my patients that we don't treat symptoms or diseases with acupuncture and Chinese herbal medicine, but we support and harmonise the body. It is difficult sometimes for patients to get their head around that concept, but instinctively they understand what I mean because, at some level, they recognise their body as being a whole structure with various subsystems.

Researchers in our field find EBM a huge challenge. My personal view is that EBM should not be rigidly imposed on Chinese medicine but rather adapted with flexibility, taking into consideration the unique characteristics of our practice and approaches. It is suggested that it may be more appropriate for Chinese medicine to adopt an efficacy-driven approach rather than the conventional mechanism-based approach.[8]

I am convinced that in the long term researchers will find a way for Chinese medicine to truly stand out with supporting evidence and, as a result, gain acceptance and respect for its great effect on human health. Until that happens, I will continue to use a combined approach in my clinic. If a patient has a scientific mind and is keen on EBM, I use it to my advantage. If they are more interested in our traditional models, I will explain my methods and treatment plan more philosophically.

TRENDING PRACTICES IN AUSTRALIA

There are many styles of practice available to a Chinese medicine practitioner, and it's up to you to decide what methods suit you best. Should you focus on acupuncture and developing a particular style in this area, or are you dedicated to becoming proficient in prescribing and dispensing herbal medicines? The following few paragraphs describe some of the modalities that are currently trending in Australia to inspire you to learn more about them and perhaps integrate one or more into your own practice.

1, 2, 3 Balance Method and Master Tung's acupuncture

The late Richard Tan's Balance Method and Master Tung's acupuncture system have both attracted many Australian aficionados in the past decade. These two systems have a classical base but diverge from the more common practice of choosing traditional point locations based on channels and local points, choosing instead to use distal or mirror points and 'extra' points identified by their originators. Personally, I have no experience with this style in practice but hear that it's very popular and effective. Because needle retention is longer with this type of treatment, it's easier to run two rooms and treat two people at the same time.

Neijing acupuncture

Neijing classical acupuncture embraces the Daoist philosophy outlined in the Huang Di Nei Jing (Yellow Emperor's Internal Classic). In Australia, there are only a few who practise this style.

Classical acupuncture differs from what is taught in undergraduate courses in that in order to achieve a tailored plan, rather than focus on pattern identification, it gives greater emphasis to the natural movement of one's qi in relation to the seasons and the environment. I am very interested in this type of practice and have taken up more studies to learn and integrate it with my classical approach in herbal medicine. This approach will take you far away from evidence-based medicine to empirical-based medicine and allows you to think just as our ancestors did.

Canonical Chinese medicine

Canonical Chinese medicine has become a developing trend in recent years. Many practitioners have a deep desire to understand the foundation of Chinese medicine, to approach treatment in the same way as our forefathers and to apply those principles unrestrictedly to current practice. It requires scholars to make ancient texts available to those who don't read Chinese. It requires certain skills to translate not only the words but the meaning of ancient texts and make this wisdom available. Luckily, we have several scholars in the West who have accomplished this task brilliantly. The best decision I made for my own practice was to study the classics such as Shang Han Lun and Jin Gui Yao Lue. My herbal practice has become a lot stronger, more predictable and a lot more confident. I am a big fan of classical medicine and love how the foundations of the five elements, the body layers and Yin and Yang come to life.

Japanese acupuncture

Acupuncture made its way to Japan through Korea in the 6th century and has been practised there since then. It's a popular style of acupuncture in Australia as there is less discomfort experienced with needle insertion. None of the Japanese styles are taught in undergraduate university courses but can be studied independently with masters skilled in the art. The main differences to Chinese style acupuncture are the size of the needles (smaller gauge), the depth of insertion (more superficial), a greater emphasis on palpation (particularly before needle insertion), a lesser focus on qi sensation and a greater incorporation of moxa and moxibustion with each treatment. My only experience of Japanese acupuncture has been at the receiving end of this gentler version of the more traditional Chinese acupuncture. If you decide to learn this style, you will join an established base of Japanese-style practitioners. Some of the Japanese masters have a big following and they offer great skills and insight to Australian practitioners.

Japanese-style herbal medicine

Kampo or Kanpō (漢方) means 'Han formula', where 'Han' refers to its Chinese origin. It was introduced to Japan from China in about 700 AD and is based on the early Chinese texts of the Han period. It evolved with time to adapt to Japanese circumstances, but the herbal formulas used closely follow the Han dynasty formulas from Shang Han Lun and Jin Gui Yao Lue. Kampo medicine is widely practised in Japan and is fully integrated into the national health care system. As I now belong to the Tian—Zheng lineage of classical herbalists, I am not certain how many Australian practitioners practise Kampo style medicine.

Abdominal acupuncture

Dr Zhiyun Bo invented a unique system of using abdominal acupuncture based on his findings of those points being important in treating a variety of conditions. His main discovery was that the prenatal or congenital channel system radiates from the umbilicus. He calls this system the Shen Que Channel System because Shen Que (acupuncture point CV8) is the Chinese term for the point on the umbilicus. Bo's Method of Abdominal Acupuncture (BMAA) was first developed in China and has found its way to Western culture in the past decade. Years ago, I completed a course in abdominal acupuncture and found it fascinating, however I have not continued to educate myself in this particular style. If there is limited access to points on the limbs or other parts of the body, then a focus on microsystems such as the abdomen works well.

Scalp acupuncture

Scalp acupuncture is a relatively new specialisation of acupuncture and was developed by Professor Ming Qing Zhu in the 1970s. The theory of scalp acupuncture is that the different areas of the brain can be stimulated by introducing acupuncture needles to appropriate areas on the scalp. By doing so, the brain function improves and reduces pain in relevant body areas. Scalp acupuncture has become a lot more popular in Australia with Chinese masters visiting our shores to share their knowledge and insight.

At the same time, Japanese practitioner Dr Toshikatsu Yamamoto developed the Yamamoto New Scalp Acupuncture (YNSA) model, a complete acupuncture microsystem of the scalp that uses basic anatomical and Ypsilon channel points to affect the bioelectric and biochemical system in order to assist patients to regain balance and health. I have no experience with this style of practice but hope to learn more about it in the near future to include it with other styles.

Auricular acupuncture

Auricular acupuncture was first invented by Dr Paul Nogier, a French scientist and physician who speculated that the whole body could be treated through activation and stimulation of certain points in the ear. I still use auricular acupuncture to assist my patients to this day. It's a great system to complement a treatment and send patients home with seeds in their ears. I acupuncture the point while they are on the table and it is perceived as very relaxing.

Korean medicine and acupuncture

Korean medicine is very similar to traditional Chinese medicine but the focus of treatment of Korean acupuncture and Korean herbal medicine is based on the constitution and body type. Korean hand acupuncture is applied as a microsystem. Integration of Korean medicine has increased since 2011 when the law in Korea changed to allow Western hospitals to install traditional Korean medicine departments with Korean doctors and vice versa. I am not familiar with this style of medicine, but I know that Korean practitioners are highly trained in both Western and Eastern styles of medicine.

Cosmetic acupuncture

Acupuncture for facial rejuvenation is a natural anti-ageing technique used to reduce fine lines and wrinkles on the face and to promote healthy skin and a radiant glow. Cosmetic acupuncture is based on using specific acupuncture points in the face and body to stimulate collagen and elastin production. The only exposure I have had to this system was in a course a few years ago with Lillian Bridges from the Lotus Institute. While I have never been interested in learning more about it, I recognise that many traditional clinics now have an acupuncturist offering cosmetic treatments.

Multi-bed acupuncture

Another trend following common practice in China is the establishment of multi-bed or community acupuncture. This model has been popularised in America by the People's Organization of Community Acupuncture (POCA). The vision of the Association of Community and Multibed Acupuncture Clinics (ACMAC) is to establish a thriving network of multi-bed acupuncture clinics providing affordable and accessible acupuncture for all. Their role is to provide training, support, peer-to-peer networking and other resources to help practitioners set up and run a multi-bed clinic. They also help spread the message so interested patients can easily locate the nearest clinic. In addition, they negotiate discounts for the supply of equipment and continuing professional development seminars, thus supporting practitioners in providing excellent treatment at reasonable prices.

This model allows patients on a limited income to receive acupuncture more than once a week. I practise in a regional area of Victoria in Australia and many people are on smaller incomes or on government benefits, so I have found multi-bed acupuncture a viable option to help my patients get the treatments they need.

Dry needling or trigger point acupuncture

Dry needling is a contentious topic in our profession because training is limited to superficial needling and does not meet the standards required to be a registered acupuncturist. To make things worse, confusion often arises between dry needling and acupuncture. In general, the training in dry needling undertaken by many health professionals who are not registered Chinese medicine practitioners can be completed in 16 hours. The exception is myotherapists who have completed a degree where they may be required to do more training, but still not to a level sufficient to be a registered acupuncturist.

Dry needling involves the application of acupuncture needles into tight, painful myofascial areas and also in locations known as 'trigger points' to release tension and obtain a healing response in these tissues. It could be compared with ashi-style acupuncture, so why call it dry needling? In Australia, the term 'acupuncturist' is a protected title restricted to registered professionals and cannot be used by a person not registered as an acupuncturist. In addition, the use of the word 'acupuncture' by a non-registered practitioner to refer to their practice is considered misleading as it tends to suggest that by practising acupuncture they must be a qualified, registered acupuncturist. This is known as 'holding out' or 'pretending' to be an acupuncturist by a person who is not registered. Therefore, the term 'dry needling' was created and also the term 'medical acupuncture', which is the term used by medical practitioners who have undertaken a short course in acupuncture and are not registered acupuncturists but are endorsed by the Medical Board of Australia.

The activities at the end of this chapter provide the opportunity for you to investigate some of the trends and modalities discussed in this section and explore those that you find most attractive to study and practice.

YOUR RESPONSIBILITIES AS A CHINESE MEDICINE PRACTITIONER

There are responsibilities that come with being a qualified and registered practitioner and it is important not only for you personally but for the entire profession that you work within the national standards and follow your obligations.

The Chinese medicine health profession's 2012 registration and its place in the National Registration and Accreditation Scheme (along with 14 other regulated health professions) is a great start in raising the profile of the profession, but registration is not the only requirement. Given the complexities of the Chinese medicine landscape and modalities, practitioners are required to follow a minimum number of rules and regulations. Read on to find out what else is important.

Australian Health Practitioner Regulation Agency (AHPRA)

The Australian Health Practitioner Regulation Agency (AHPRA) supports the 15 health profession National Boards, of which the Chinese Medicine Board of Australia (CMBA) is one, in their role of protecting the public and setting standards and policies that all registered health practitioners must meet. AHPRA and the National Boards work together to register health practitioners and, when required, investigate complaints or concerns regarding health practitioners.

Chinese Medicine Board of Australia (CMBA)

Chinese medicine commenced registration on 1 July 2012. In order to practise legally in Australia today, you must register with the CMBA (www.chinesemedicineboard.gov.au) once you have completed your education with an approved program. This regulating entity is one of 15 National Boards representing each of the 15 registered health professions (including the medical profession). The CMBA's primary responsibility is to safeguard the public. Students can register with the CMBA for free.

The CMBA regulates the practice of Chinese medicine and practitioners are expected to comply with its guidelines and are held responsible if the guidelines have been disregarded. The board's functions include developing standards, codes and guidelines for the profession; approving accreditation standards and programs of study; and assessing applications for registration as a Chinese medicine practitioner in the three divisions of acupuncture, Chinese herbal medicine and dispensing. This includes applications from overseas trained practitioners wanting to practise in Australia. The CMBA also investigates complaints and sanctions practitioners if they are non-compliant with guidelines, fail to work according to the expected standard or have breached the *Code of conduct*. They may refer matters to disciplinary hearings.

First and foremost, the CMBA is supported by AHPRA, and both are governed by the Health Practitioner Regulation National Law Act 2009 enforced in each state and territory. There is sometimes a misconception about the function of the CMBA. Even though the board shares many of our values, it does not and must not lobby for practitioners. This belongs in the remit of professional associations instead. I consider registration with the CMBA to be an advantage because it lifts standards and puts the profession on the map of health care, therefore strengthening the position of Chinese medicine as an industry.

CMBA Code of conduct and guidelines

The CMBA has published a *Code of conduct* that is sensible and easy to follow. Most of the principles are consistent for all the registered health professions. They include relevant ethics such as only working within your area of training, obtaining informed consent and maintaining professional boundaries (eg. not engaging in a relationship with patients).

Practitioners are bound by the CMBA *Code of conduct* and additionally the code of conduct established by their chosen professional association. This is not to make life difficult but to foster high standards in both practitioner care and in the operation of a health care business.

Remember, any patient has the right to ask for a copy of their patient file and you should be able to accede to that request promptly. If you don't complete the patient record at the time of the appointment because you have been busy, called away or distracted in some way, make a point (and stick to it) of completing it as soon as practicable. Knowing that your patient might have access to those records, and in some circumstances an insurance company or legal representative could also read them, you must ensure that the information in patient files is impartial and has used their words to describe certain situations or emotions, rather than your interpretation of it.

Other laws

Several Acts come into play that are the basis of regulation of the Chinese medicine profession. What is an Act? It starts as a bill which becomes law once it passes through the various legislative steps and is approved.

One Act that will touch your professional life is the Therapeutic Goods Act (1989), which is administered by the Therapeutic Goods Administration (TGA). The TGA regulates medical devices/ instruments and medicines including nutritional supplements and some herbal medicines. The Australian Minister for Health has responsibility for this Act.

Manufacturers are expected to follow the principles and procedures of Good Manufacturing Practice (GMP) to ensure that therapeutic goods are of high quality. These guidelines extend beyond manufacturing standards to labelling and packaging. All pre-packed and over-the-counter medicines require listing or registration with the Australian Register of Therapeutic Goods (ARTG) and require an Australian sponsor who maintains those listings or registrations.

Guidelines for safe Chinese herbal medicine practice

With the establishment of the CMBA's *Guidelines for safe Chinese herbal medicine practice*, there are specific requirements for prescribing, dispensing and labelling herbs. These herbal dispensing guidelines are the minimum standards required to run a practice that is both safe and professional. They are discussed in more detail in Element 4: 'Prescribing and dispensing herbs'.

If herbs are scheduled within the TGA's *Standard for the Uniform Scheduling of Medicines and Poisons (SUSMP)* then the restrictions for those herbs have to be followed religiously. Schedule 10 (previously Appendix C) of the SUSMP lists herbs that we currently have no access to; it is illegal to handle, manage, dispense or sell those herbs.

Reporting suspected adverse effects to the TGA

Under the CMBA's *Code of conduct* and *Guidelines for safe Chinese herbal medicine practice*, registered Chinese medicine practitioners are expected to report adverse events. There is an easy-to-complete online notification form on the CMBA website for this purpose. Any untoward medical occurrence in a patient arising from a medicine, even if it does not necessarily have a causal relationship with this medicine, is described as an adverse event. All reports are prioritised according to their risks. Any individual can report side effects, but all registered professions are encouraged to do so.

The TGA will record the information, including relevant medical history, laboratory results and how the adverse event was treated. Each report is given a unique ID number so that further information can be added later on. The information contained in the database assists the TGA in establishing and identifying safety signals (flags). If there is a safety concern, the TGA will instigate a detailed evaluation. Three months after the initial report is made, the information is transferred to the Database of Adverse Event Notifications (DAEN), which is accessible by the public.

As a registered profession, there is a need for us to work professionally. As prescribers, suppliers, sponsors or dispensers of medicines, we must act responsibly. Bear in mind that these reports are not about blame but are for the purpose of accruing knowledge.

Other relevant guidelines

Other useful guidelines by the CMBA, including guidelines for advertising regulated health services and guidelines for mandatory notifications, can be found on the CMBA website at www.chinesemedicineboard.gov.au/codes-guidelines.aspx.

I recommend checking the CMBA website on a regular basis as existing policies are revised and new ones developed. The CMBA consults widely on all policies affecting the profession. A useful prompt is the 'News' page at www.chinesemedicineboard.gov.au/News.aspx.

Public liability and professional indemnity insurance

Before commencing practice, you need to ensure you have adequate insurance cover in effect. Public liability insurance covers injuries to patients, clients or members of the public on your premises. In comparison, professional indemnity insurance (PII) protects you and your business in the circumstance of claims of alleged negligence or breach of duty arising from an act, error or omission in the performance of professional services. This insurance is required for all registered health professionals and is designed to cover the risks arising from a health practitioner's provision of health care goods and services to the public.

The Health Practitioner Regulation National Law (the National Law) requires National Boards to develop a registration standard on the requirements for PII arrangements for health practitioners registered in the profession. Section 129 of the National Law provides that a registered health practitioner must not practise unless they have appropriate PII arrangements in effect. The PII arrangements registration standard that all Chinese medicine practitioners should comply with is available on the CMBA website. A practitioner must notify the CMBA within seven days if they no longer have appropriate PII arrangements in place that meet the requirements of this standard.

Insurance cover can be arranged independently with the insurance company of your choice or with the insurance company recommended by your professional association (usually at a reduced premium). In the past, I have obtained quotes from other insurance companies but always found them to be more expensive than policies offered through the professional association. Whichever is the case for you, make sure that you negotiate an appropriate policy with an approved insurer.

For insurance purposes you must disclose the modalities you practise. It can affect your premium and your actual cover if you do not fully disclose your scope of practice to the insurance provider. If you add new modalities, inform your insurer to be sure that the modality is included in your cover in the eventuality of anything going wrong. As much as you don't want to invest too much money in your insurance premium, it is not worth the risk to compromise or take shortcuts with your insurance policy.

Australian Business Number

An Australian Business Number (ABN) is a unique 11-digit number that identifies you as an Australian business. To be eligible for an ABN, you must have started trading or have undertaken business-like activities in Australia. If you are seeking a paid position, you won't need to apply for an ABN, but you need one if you are you are an independent contractor or sole trader. You can apply for an ABN free of charge on the Australian Government Business Registration Service website.

Choose a business name or keep it in your own name. Be mindful that if you decide to change the name later, you will have to complete a business name transfer. From experience, the preference for business names can change over time as you develop and progress as a practitioner and have more clarity about exactly what you offer to your patients. A simple name that is easily understood by prospects is good.

Joining a professional association

There are various professional associations operating in Australia that you can join. In our industry, the main organisations are membership based. Some associations represent Chinese medicine only while others represent a number of health professions.

The CMBA regulates practitioners under statute and its focus is to protect the public, while the role of a professional association (also called a professional body, professional organisation or professional society) is to represent the interests of its industry members and advance the profession. It is expected that a professional association will have the strength and resources to lobby on behalf of the profession when required to do so. Most will also offer professional development for their members.

Other benefits include reduced PII premiums through arrangements with insurance providers, as well as easier access to health fund claiming, which can be extremely onerous to organise on your own (see further details on health funds below). By joining a professional association and taking advantage of such benefits, practitioners will get better outcomes and funds will be spent where they are most needed.

I encourage you to join the first association on the list below as it has supported the profession for several decades and puts all its money towards doing so.

- **Australian Acupuncture and Chinese Medicine Association (AACMA)**
  - » Represents Chinese medicine practitioners only
  - » Reduced student and new graduate fees
  - » www.acupuncture.org.au

- **Australian Natural Therapists Association (ANTA)**
  - » Represents Chinese medicine practitioners and other natural medicine modalities
  - » Reduced student fees
  - » www.australiannaturaltherapistsassociation.com.au

- **Australian Traditional-Medicine Society (ATMS)**
  - » Represents Chinese medicine practitioners and other natural medicine modalities
  - » Reduced student fees
  - » www.atms.com.au

- **Chinese Medicine & Acupuncture Society of Australia (CMASA)**
  - » Represents Chinese medicine practitioners and remedial massage therapists
  - » Reduced student fees
  - » www.australiantcm.com.au/cmasaNew/about.php

- **Chinese Medicine Health Alliance (CMHA)**
  - » Legal representation for the Chinese medicine profession in Australia
  - » Encouraging unity and collaboration of the industry in Australia
  - » www.chinesemedicinehealthalliance.com.au

- **Chinese Medicine Industry Council of Australia (CMIC)**
  - » Represents manufacturers, sponsors and dispensers of Chinese medicine
  - » www.cmic-aus.org.au

- **Federation of Chinese Medicine & Acupuncture Societies of Australia Ltd (FCMA)**

>> Represents Chinese medicine practitioners only

>> Reduced student fees

>> www.fcma.org.au

- **Traditional Medicine of China Society Australia (TMCSA)**

>> Represents Chinese medicine practitioners only

>> www.tmcsa.stcm.com.au

Medibank provider number and private insurance claiming

One of the main reasons for a practitioner to become a member of a professional association is to be granted health provider status by health funds so that patients can claim rebates. Rather than applying for recognition with each health fund individually, being a member of an association gains recognition with all health funds.

For the installation of a HICAPS or Tyro terminal, you must have a provider number with Medibank Private. Make sure you offer your patients the full benefit of their private health insurance at your clinic and have a HICAPS or Tyro terminal installed; all claims are done on the spot which saves you and your patients' ample time and offers great convenience to your patients.

Print and complete the following application form to apply for your provider number: www.medibank.com.au/content/dam/retail/providers/Provider_Application_form.pdf

It takes about three weeks to receive the provider number, so it's best to start the process early. If you will be practising from several locations, you need to apply for a different provider number for each location.

Continuing professional development (CPD)

Registered practitioners have a professional obligation under the National Law to complete a minimum of 20 hours of continuing professional development (CPD) per year. A minimum of four hours must relate to professional issues and the remaining hours spent on suitable activities to maintain and improve competence in the profession.

Professional issues are topics relating to regulatory or administrative issues, marketing, advertising, ethical standards, codes and guidelines, infection control, informed consent, privacy and other regulatory matters. Clinical matters can include research, case studies, practical experience or academic theory. In other words, topics that can improve your clinical practice, broaden your knowledge and expertise, expand competence and develop your abilities personally and professionally are suitable.

Of the 20 CPD hours, at least 14 must include formal learning activities. The remaining hours can be on informal activities which must also be well documented and properly justified. Of course, you can attend as many CPD activities as you like, with 20 hours being the minimum requirement.

The CMBA *Continuing professional development guidelines* provides examples of formal and informal activities to help you choose appropriate courses, seminars and workshops. A current first aid certificate (HLTFA301B or equivalent) is part of your obligation with the CMBA and any of the professional associations. First aid training providers may offer courses in your area on a regular basis or, alternatively, you can find courses via St John Ambulance Australia or the Australian Red Cross.

I plan my CPD at least 12 months ahead and choose courses, seminars and workshops strategically. I don't wait until the last minute to top up my points for the year. Once I decide on the skills I want to focus on, I set out to find courses that are suitable and conducive to the topics I am interested in. You can deduct the costs of CPD from your tax as it's a part of your yearly cost to maintain registration. Attending professional development activities in person or online is also a great opportunity to catch up with like-minded individuals.

The CPD year starts on 1 December and ends on 30 November in line with the registration year. Some professional associations follow this too while others follow the Australian financial year from 1 July to 30 June. It is advisable to maintain a detailed record of the nature of the event, the topic, the number of hours, the presenter, etc. The CMBA requires only that you make a statutory declaration attesting to completion of the required CPD activities when you re-register each year. Random audits, however, are conducted. Some professional associations also operate in this way, while others (such as AACMA) require members to submit their CPD record annually.

As AHPRA (on behalf of the national boards), professional associations and health funds periodically audit CPD obligations, it is essential not only to maintain good records but also to meet all the criteria. For the latest CPD requirements (and other information on codes and guidelines), please visit www.chinesemedicineboard.gov. au/Codes-Guidelines.aspx

CPD requirements are only one side of the coin. As you progress on your path to becoming a successful practitioner, you will continually develop as an individual. Constantly screening and scanning your skills and knowledge for areas that need addressing is being honest and transparent with yourself and shows a high level of self-reflection. Once you identify areas that need improvement, you can choose CPD activities accordingly.

When selecting CPD activities you might also consider:

- the qualifications, credentials and experience of the provider

- selecting a range of topics and activities over time

- choosing activities that are consistent with the Board's other standards and guidelines.

The CMBA guidelines do not say that you are limited to four hours on professional issues. You might feel you would benefit from more. If you feel the need to spend more time on the logistics of your practice, diving deeper into patient rapport or studying the guidelines for good dispensing practices by the World Health Organization (WHO)[9], then that's what you focus on. However, you still need to spend a minimum of 16 hours on issues specific to Chinese medicine clinical practice.

Planning your CPD activities in advance

If you are clear in your vision and have the appropriate learning goals to ensure you are heading in the right direction, then it is best to find CPD activities that are aligned with your path. Many activities are advertised several months in advance, so January is a good month to sit down and think about your 20 hours of professional development. Where will you spend your time, energy and money to support your professional development over the coming months? You may only have six months left if your professional associations require your CPD details by the end of June.

Which style or styles of acupuncture have you embraced and what are the means to make you confident with it? What activities are available – and if not available, how could you arrange them? What new skills are you attracted to and how can you make them yours? Which practitioners most inspire you and how do they run their practice? You could ask to spend time with them to find out if what they do would suit you. If you plan, you will achieve. Instead of choosing the route of elimination, choose the deliberate and more direct route of strategic achieving.

> If you plan, you will achieve.

BRINGING YOUR AUTHENTIC STYLE INTO PRACTICE

The beauty of being a Chinese medicine practitioner is that you have a safe and established body of wisdom and you can bring your own essence into your individual style of practice. When I look at how I practise today, I know it's an expression of who I am. It reflects my life experiences, everything I have studied with various teachers, my past experience during 17 years of practice and the way I express myself with others through both speech and body language.

For you to bring your essence into your practice, you need to accumulate all your knowledge and wisdom – practical and theoretical – into one package and apply that every day. Sound easy? It should be. Perhaps you could start by sitting down and writing your life story. Where did you start, where did it take you and where are you now? What have you learnt from all of this? Which teachers at school, college or university left an impression on you? What things caught your attention that you were impressed with? What are your friends doing that inspires you? And what things are you trying to avoid, not because you fear them, but because you have seen or experienced that they are not a reflection of your true self or they are something that got you into trouble in the past?

Chinese medicine will help you to progress, simply by its very nature. For example, there are two ways to look at the principles of Yin and Yang – a simple way or a complex way. Once you start looking beyond simplicity and start to break things down further into fragments, it becomes complex. What I mean is that Chinese medicine is simple but at the same time there is a depth to it. Without any doubt, progress is imminent once you start working with it. You have to start somewhere. Start where you are today.

I encourage you to use the well-established principles of Chinese medicine first and practise those basics for some time so that you understand how they work. Make sure you use them exactly as they are meant to be applied. Only then should you look at an extension of those principles. It is essential to our medicine to apply the method as it has been done for thousands of years. It is vital for our medicine to endure and stay alive and not be diluted with immature newly invented concepts.

> Developing your own style is something that grows over time.

Developing your own style is something that grows over time. It is personal and an organic process. If you have established your values and goals ahead of starting your practice, it becomes a more linear development than it would be if you had no sense of where you want to go. This is a reminder of how important it is to have a goal, which automatically leads to a path with your values accompanying the process all the way.

WHAT DO YOU OFFER?

Be clear on what type of services you will offer before you start looking for a location. For example, are you offering acupuncture and Chinese medicine consultation alone or are you combining it with other modalities? Will you offer each modality separately or combine them depending on what your patient needs?

I offer an initial consultation that includes an acupuncture treatment at a higher cost and longer duration than a herbal consultation only. If my patients choose the initial acupuncture consultation, I make sure I have enough time to apply all the treatments needed for the best outcome (ie. acupuncture, cupping and moxibustion). If I recommend that they take herbs as well, I will spend time working out the herbal formula best suited for their presenting complaint.

Various aspects to consider when deciding on treatment time and cost include:

- welcoming the patient
- making sure they are comfortable
- talking about their problem and the reason for their visit
- completing their initial consultation form (on paper or electronically)
- assessing results of any previous medical tests and investigations
- taking pulses
- conducting other palpation such as abdominal diagnosis
- coming up with a diagnosis and working out a treatment plan
- communicating the treatment plan (perhaps writing it down)

- getting consent for treatment (even though they have signed it on the intake form)
- explaining how particular treatments work
- explaining your findings and hence your treatment approach
- assessing diet and lifestyle and discussing your recommendations for modifications
- explaining herbs
- determining the appropriate herbal formula
- dispensing or ordering prescriptions
- carrying out treatment
- taking payment and booking the next appointment
- farewelling the patient.

Even when first starting out you need to be in charge of the consultation and manage your time well. I tended to treat only one side (front or back) in my initial consultations of one hour. My clinic has now only recently brought in a longer initial consultation of 75 minutes (at a higher charge) to accommodate complex conditions or to allow more time with a particular patient.

Say you decide to make your initial consultation to be a duration of 60 minutes. If the patient arrives early (which I ask all my new patients to do to complete paperwork), the consultation starts once you take them through to the treatment room. I take an average of 20–25 minutes to establish a full medical history and diagnosis for the patient's problem. The initial consultation is important to start building rapport with the patient, so ensure you allow enough time for this. Building patient rapport will be covered in more detail in Element 4: 'Practical techniques and tools to keep you on track'.

If the patient has not had experience with acupuncture or Chinese herbal medicine before, it is important to brief them thoroughly so that by the time they are on the table they are confident, relaxed, informed and have given consent to be treated. According to the

CMBA *Code of conduct* (section 3.5): "Informed consent is a person's voluntary decision about healthcare that is made with knowledge and understanding of the benefits and risks involved". In order to give informed consent, it is important that the patient understands exactly what is going to happen during the consultation.

Follow-up appointments can be shorter. If I am only treating a shoulder or a knee, I make a 45-minute follow-up consultation. If the condition is more complex (eg. fertility, menopause, digestive problems, exhaustion, anxiety) or involves multiple conditions, or if a patient tends to ask a lot of questions and likes detailed explanations, I will book them for a longer follow-up appointment of 60 minutes.

Time it and trial it

Working under pressure can be exhilarating but it can be detrimental as well, so it's good to sit down and think about these factors before you start. As you gain experience and new skills you might change some aspects of your treatments, however it is advisable to keep your treatments as consistent as possible. To finetune time management, I suggest you trial run your planned appointments with family or friends. If you role-play and time appointments now, you will have a lot more confidence with timing when it counts.

Starting treatment about 25 minutes into the consultation will allow approximately 25 minutes with the needles in place (which is really all that's needed). Following removal of the needles, you should have ample time to take payment, rebook them and answer any last questions they might have before they leave. If you are fortunate enough to have a receptionist, it is nice to accompany your patient to the reception area and leave them in the hands of the receptionist.

Your income is important

When determining your fees you will need to take several factors into consideration. The main consideration is that you must charge a fee that covers your costs and also earns you a living. If you don't do that, you will go broke and stop practising. You also need to feel valued by what you charge and get a sense of a fair exchange. Medicare and other subsidies are not applicable to the Chinese medicine industry so it is necessary to generate an adequate income.

The location of your practice might give some indication as to what to charge for your sessions. However, I have heard practitioners say that they charge the highest in less affluent areas and still have a busy practice. In my regional area, I charge reasonably and we can now accommodate individuals with a lower income at a more affordable rate in our multi-bed acupuncture space.

Sometimes you might want to consider a patient's disposable income as financial constraints can be an issue. If I discover during the initial appointment that a patient is on a pension or unemployment benefits, I will either offer them a shorter appointment or refer them to the community acupuncture sessions. But I never assume that they don't have enough money to pay for their optimal treatment plan, which may include herbal medicines and several treatments each week.

WHERE TO SET UP PRACTICE

Once you have established what your focus will be and how you are going to work, you can decide where you are going to offer your expertise. Should you initially work from home, rent a room, become a contractor, open your own clinic (and should you do that alone or with someone else?), or find employment in another enterprise?

If you have already thought about what services you are going to offer, the decision on where to offer your services may be easier. If you are still not sure what services you are going to offer, you might ponder the question of where you are going to work first and consequently develop a better idea on how you are going to work.

When I first migrated to Australia, I decided to work in a local multidisciplinary practice that offered Bowen therapy, remedial massage, relaxation massage, naturopathy and personal training. It gave me an opportunity to learn about running a business in

Australia, ease my way into treating Australian patients and find out more about the local demography. I also made lots of valuable contacts for referrals and friends. This situation worked really well for me and, being the only acupuncturist in our area, I quickly built my patient base.

Following are various options for setting up practice, with the pros and cons of each.

Working from home

You have extra space at home with a nice, quiet room that is suitable for treatments. That's great. I know some practitioners who love working from home. It's generally low in outgoings (eg. rent and utilities) and you can claim tax rebates on home office expenses. Generally, you will have only one or two rooms for treatments, but working from home has the advantage of allowing you to attend to other things when you are not in consultation with patients. Much depends on the layout of your home and on your personal circumstances.

I worked from home for three years at one stage because I could not find a professional space in my area that I liked. I had no waiting or reception area which caused issues when patients did not arrive on time for their appointments. If the space had been separated from the main part of my home with its own entrance and no access to the rest of the house, I could see it working much better. A separate toilet facility would also be an advantage so that patients are not using your private bathroom or toilet.

Personal security is another consideration. Consider the fact that you would be letting people into your home who you have never met before, whose background you don't know and who have literally just walked in from the street. The display of my private life also bothered me as I lived in a small community.

Flowing from those concerns, you need to decide how best to advertise your business and what contact details you will use.

Will everyone contact you first by telephone or email so that you can obtain some basic information for potential screening before booking them in?

Financially, there are different tax liabilities for those who work in a home that they own as opposed to renting. Capital gains tax applies if you are using your home as a business. It's best to talk to an accountant or the Australian Taxation Office if you need clarification.

If you decide to start working from home, remember to take precautions and be well organised as it's very important to be professional with people's health and wellbeing. Keep the following suggestions in mind:

- Make sure that your space looks inviting while still meeting professional standards, including the CMBA guidelines.

- Keep the space clean, tidy and well aired.

- Make sure that you have a backup plan if something unexpected or undesirable happens so you are not going to be out of your depth (eg. you could have a phone on you at all times) including working out an escape path.

- Be aware that some patients might arrive early or late so it is best to have a waiting area prepared. Patients sometimes bring along their children, partner or parents, so make sure there is space for several people.

Based on my own experience, I consider working from home to be a great short-term option but, despite the costs that can be saved in outgoings, I don't consider it the best option unless you live in a house that is purpose-built to accommodate a clinic or can be easily modified. It might have a separate entrance or a separate studio, and ideally it needs a separate bathroom or toilet that is only for patient use. In addition, it requires an adequate waiting area to accommodate several people coming to the clinic at the same time. Consider whether you have ever come across a medical practitioner, a chiropractor, an osteopath or a physiotherapist who works from home? I haven't, and I live in regional Victoria where the chances of this are greater.

Renting a room in a business

Another option is to rent a room in an established business. This means that you promote and run your own practice out of someone else's premises. Often you will manage your own bookings, administer your own payments and promote your own business activities while operating from premises that are not primarily dedicated to Chinese medicine. This could be a room in a pharmacy, a massage business or the clinic of an osteopath or chiropractor. It could even be a room attached to a hairdresser or beauty therapist or any other space that is available in another business.

This option is most appealing if you are able to team up with an enterprise that aligns with what you do and with your values and goals. After all, you are offering a medical service treating patients with often severe conditions, so do you really want to tell them that you work in the back room of a hairdressing salon? As much as the perfect space isn't always available right away, it is better to plan ahead and look for an appropriate space to work from early on and not wait until you have graduated and want to start your practice.

This option is suitable for graduates who don't mind promoting their services. As you will require cards and flyers, and possibly advertisements, a website and social media, you will have to be savvy and prepared to spend some money. It's less expensive than setting up your own clinic, however, so could be a good option if you find a space and business that you like.

If you decide to start working from someone else's business by renting a room, you should address the following areas:

- Make sure the business you choose aligns with your philosophy and your expectations of location, design and complementary modalities offered.

- Try to have a look at it from your prospective patients' view: Will they find you there easily? Can they associate the services that you offer with the other products or services offered? Will they perceive your service in a medical sense?

- Make sure there is a good collaboration between you, the business owner and other service providers in those premises.

- Ensure that you have a basic contract in place as this will help to clarify mutual expectations.

Working as a contractor

Let us look at the subcontractor situation, which I consider one of the better options – especially if the business you're contracting to is a Chinese medicine clinic. But this needs to be set up properly, so the arrangement is not considered as sham contracting which can attract huge fines.[10]

As a subcontractor, you can embrace a team and hopefully it embraces you in return. The business will already have an established patient base. Patients will be referred to you and there is often an opportunity to do locum work when other practitioners are on leave or call in sick. You can discuss treatment plans for patients, tricky cases, share notes, exchange knowledge of effective techniques and muse about how to better manage patients who are hard to handle. As a new practitioner, it is important to have guidance from more experienced practitioners, as this will help in building your confidence more quickly and in setting up a path of greater success.

> It is important to have guidance from more experienced practitioners.

At the time of writing, the rate for subcontractors is anything between 50% and 70%. This means you will be paid $50–$70 for any treatment costing $100. It usually also means that you don't have to do anything: a receptionist accepts payments, issues receipts and makes appointments, bookings are taken care of and, often, towels, needles and other supplies are provided. All you have to do is step in and work. It sounds good, doesn't it? The downside is that, despite the advantages, some practitioners feel a level of dissatisfaction with the payment level, especially if remuneration is only 50% of what the patient pays.

Another difficulty is the distribution of clients when you first start out. What if your first patient is booked for 9.00am and the next one is not until 4.30pm? What are you going to do in the meantime? This is especially tricky if you live a long way from the clinic. And would you feel comfortable working at a multidisciplinary clinic where you are the only Chinese medicine practitioner? As a new graduate, you might find it difficult unless you have previously worked with the team – for example, if you worked with them as a massage therapist and have now completed your degree and have started working as a Chinese medicine practitioner.

I worked in this model for two years (shortly after I migrated to Australia) and it helped me establish a client base. It can work well for a new graduate too. I was working in a business that offered massage, Bowen therapy and fitness training. Thanks to cross-referrals, I was able to build my own practice quickly and it helped that I was the only Chinese medicine practitioner in the area. At the time, I had to provide my own equipment and linen, and also clean the rooms each time I finished a shift. But the fact that they offered reception services was a bonus.

I have found that this model can work successfully in the short term. In the long term, there seems to be a level of dissatisfaction from both parties. It is not really the optimal situation when starting up, because if you leave it is likely you will have to start from scratch and build your clientele again. We all know that the initial phase of creating momentum in the practice can take a bit of time. However, it can get you into the workforce, provide you with experience and confidence, and make you think about a system (your own framework).

If you decide to work as a subcontractor in an established business, think about the following:

- Look at the conditions of the contract carefully. Is it up to you to generate new patients or will the business do that?

- How many of your ideas can you bring into the existing business?

- Make sure you meet all the other practitioners working there and find out their experience.

- Are you planning to work in this manner for a long time or simply to get your foot in the door and gain experience in practising and running a business? It's good to have transparency around that.

- The expectation is that you will be treating the clinic's patients, not your own, which you need to be comfortable with.

Being an employee

How about being part of a real team, having your hours or shifts organised, working from an established business and having a salary? This could be an optimal start for you and can offer a very professional approach. It's so much easier than working out a percentage that's fair. It is important to note, however, that "Unlike many other professions within the health care industry, there are few salaried employment opportunities for CM".[11]

My Safflower clinic has recently taken on two other practitioners. We negotiated their number of hours per week and used the Fair Work Commission's Health Professionals and Support Services Award to calculate their salary.[12] This also allowed us to offer a paid introduction and training program. Each practitioner is part of the team and aligns themselves with our goals and values. On days when there are fewer patients, we can assign other jobs to them, such as research, event organisation, the creation of patient resources or marketing activities. Working as part of a well-defined and organised team has great advantages over the potential isolation of solo practice where all decisions are made alone, especially at the most critical time of transition from student to practitioner.

If you decide to find employment in an established business, think about the following:

- A contract comes with responsibilities for both you and your employer. Are you prepared to establish yourself under the given circumstances?

- Do you share the same values with the business that is planning to employ you?

- Are you good at team collaboration?

- Do you mind working with instructions and guidance? Or do you prefer to make your own decisions about everything?

- Does your employer provide you with training or mentoring?

- Are you paid under an award? If so, which one?

- Does your employer pay your superannuation?

- Is there a performance review mechanism in place?

Opening your own clinic

Opening your own clinic space in commercial premises with a shopfront will be more challenging when first starting out unless you have prepared for this in advance. Alternatively, you might already be working as an allied health practitioner and so are able to simply integrate your new skills into your business. But if you are newly renting a whole space, the monthly payments of rent and utilities can be daunting. You will be looking at rent, insurance, utilities (water, electricity), council/shire rates and other costs to promote your new business.

Setting up your own clinic takes your practice to another level. It's not like operating from home where you could decide one day that you don't want to do it anymore and simply move on. You will be required to sign contracts for the lease, utilities, etc. Also, the space you find might not suit the way you want to set up your clinic. There will be a significant financial investment before you start working and generating income. It's important that you look at signage and promotional materials as well.

It's not an easy decision to make and you might lose some sleep over patient numbers suddenly declining. Or you might worry that the patient base might not grow as fast as needed. Sadly, statistics show that over 60% of small businesses in Australia don't make it past the first three years, mainly due to lack of capital and lack of business training.[13]

Running your own business is not a piece of cake. There will be times when you run out of energy while you multitask with setting up and promoting your business, treating patients and keeping an eye on your finances. Paid holiday is no longer an option – at least not in the beginning – and some days it simply might not be possible to leave your work behind at the door when you come home.

The great advantage is that you will be able to set up the space exactly as you like it and infuse your essence, your ideas and your philosophy into it. So, if you are the type of person who doesn't mind challenges and you have a clear idea on how you are going to make it happen, go for it.

You will do much better if you have some business training or bring people into your business who can help you run it. Also, be prepared to have some capital on the side. It is devastating to fail and, although I don't wish to discourage you, it is important to be clear that while setting up your own clinic is exciting it does require focus, energy and resilience.

FLYING SOLO... OR NOT?

In deciding where to first set up practice or work, remember your long-term scenario. Make informed decisions now and put steps in place to achieve it. Tap into your vision. Where do you want to be in 12 months, 3 years or 10 years?

Where do you want to be in 12 months, 3 years or 10 years?

If you make an informed decision as to your preferred style of business practice, you will get more out of it in the long term and won't have to waste a significant amount of time and energy discovering what best suits your personality.

The following table provides a snapshot of some pros and cons of each working model.

Business model	Personality type	Business expertise required	Money required	Timeline
Contractor	Happy to fit in	Minimal	None	Mid-term
Renting a space	A little independent	Some	Some	Long-term
Employment	Happy to fit in	Minimal	None	Mid-term
Own clinic	Highly independent	Significant	Significant	Long-term

If you are envisaging flying solo, it is best to prepare early. There will be extra costs and a lot more energy needed to organise your space. Be clear, concise and realistic about embarking on your own practice after graduating and your expectations in terms of its progress.

Consider the following to help you make this important decision:

- Are you self-motivated and driven?

- Do you have experience in running a business? Do you have experience negotiating with real estate agents, council, suppliers, builders, graphic designers, printers and more?

- Are you good with numbers and budgeting?

- Are you prepared to invest a minimum of two years into running your own clinic space and financing it?

- Do you have good and consistent energy levels so that you can attend to all the tasks required?

- Are you good with managing time?

- Do you have a clear vision about your own space?

- Do you have a clear and concise idea on how to attract patients and the confidence to accomplish that?

- Do you have systems and measures in place to help you?

- Do you have a network in place for support?

- Are you aware of what the law requires you to do?

- Do you have a plan for signage?

- Is there enough parking space available at the premises?

Of course, there is scope to team up with someone equally keen to set up shop. If you choose a business partner, it is important to be clear about what is expected of each of you. Is someone responsible for one area and the other person for another? Who is managing finances, marketing, administration and cleaning? Who will negotiate with your suppliers, your real estate agent, your bank and other businesses that are going to be involved?

If you are starting out solo and are inexperienced in running your own business, make sure that you train yourself in good business practices or find a mentor or a coach who has the expertise and can guide you. Be aware that it requires resilience and focus to get your own business going. Additionally, it requires a lot of resources, both energy and money. Make sure that you are financially covered for at least two years when starting out.

LOOKING AFTER YOURSELF

It's easy to become isolated as a Chinese medicine practitioner as you are by yourself when consulting with patients. It doesn't matter where you work. This can be daunting at times and some potentially uncomfortable situations could arise. Your patient might be super difficult to deal with; you might have a really low energy day and find it hard to communicate or express yourself; you could have a difficult situation at home or with your family; or you might be worried about your finances, your success rate or the state of the planet in general.

Staying connected is about honouring self in order that you can thrive as a Chinese medicine practitioner and bring about health and wellbeing. There are two aspects – connection with self while connecting with others. It is only when there is room for this to happen that we can be the best we can be and so be a role model to our patients, bringing the rich traditions of Chinese medicine into a contemporary lifestyle.

I still notice at times that I give recommendations to my patients to help them live a well-balanced life and then realise that I don't walk the talk myself. You are the judge of your own balance and you need to keep your finger on your own pulse. Constantly – and I *mean* constantly – assess whether things are going well for you and whether you are feeling like you 'should'.

If the flow is inhibited and you feel stuck, discuss this with colleagues or mentors and work out the necessary actions to get you back on track. Don't let it go for too long. Take action early and perhaps pencil in some days off to give you space to breathe and care for yourself. Allow yourself to find solutions to your problems early on. Look out for the signs: you feel fatigued or low-spirited; your body is in pain or discomfort; the sharpness and clarity have gone in your consultations; you are starting to withdraw and don't want to see or deal with patients; or you are not feeling enriched or inspired anymore.

Surround yourself with people you want in your life and make an extra effort to cultivate those connections. The way you apply this differs from patients to personal friends to suppliers or any other people involved with your business. We will talk more about maintaining connections for your business in Element 3: 'Connecting with your community'.

> ## Develop a deep relationship with yourself and others.

I encourage you to develop a deep relationship with yourself and others so that you can practise optimally and seamlessly. Finding the perfect balance requires your constant attention. It will be challenging for you if you are not busy enough and taxing if you are too busy. To align your practice with your goals, give a lot of thought to how many patients you are consulting each week, fortnight or month. If the aim is to see 40 people in three days, then you have to accommodate 13–14 treatments in one day. With ample energy it won't be a problem, but when starting out, this might be an overzealous plan.

When I teach myself to stay grounded, I ultimately teach myself to be me. A balanced me. I find this to be more and more important as the world around becomes busier. Instead of wasting time, energy and words on gossiping or engaging in negative actions, I will walk in nature, play with my dog, or read something that stimulates and inspires me. I have discovered that this is a good way for me to maintain my equanimity and it helps me in clinic as I listen to the troubles and tribulations of my patients. The longer I work as a practitioner, the more important it has become. Keeping my finger on my own pulse means that I am keeping myself on track. As I know myself best and respect my abilities, I can work more effectively.

I encourage you to think about your self-care plan and what it includes. It's not always easy to know what's best for us, but remember... it's often small things that make a big difference. To find the perfect balance, you need to consider carefully what actions or non-actions should be included in your life.

ELEMENTAL SELF-CARE

Self-care is not selfish. In our profession, self-care is essential. If you have a tendency to bottle things up, find a counsellor or other trained professional who you can talk to once a month or more frequently if you feel the need. Or you could share any difficulties with a mentor or a trusted colleague. It's hard to share what moves us in clinic with family as it could overstep patient confidentiality and also interfere with family relationships.

I remember I had a patient with a very upsetting experience and I was so moved by her story that it was hard not to think about it all the time. I chose to talk to a counsellor about it for a bit of a debrief. I realised that I wasn't prepared for a situation like that which caught me by surprise. I now talk things through as it helps me to process them and I do that best with a psychology trained professional.

ELEMENT 2 ACTIVITIES

These activities will assist you in working through the complex and diverse content of this Element. Please make sure you spend ample time working through them.

2.1: Practise explaining EBM with Chinese medicine principles

1. Download a copy of *The Acupuncture Evidence Project* from the AACMA website and familiarise yourself with the eight conditions with most evidence for efficacy.
2. Think about the causative factors of those conditions according to Chinese medicine.
3. Explain the causative factors and resulting patterns to a colleague or friend.

2.2: Adding more skills

4. Spend an hour or so investigating some of the current trends in treatment methods.
5. Create a shortlist of the top three that you find most attractive to explore further.
6. Check websites and live seminars offered in the next 12 months and book time to learn about those techniques.

2.3: Code of conduct familiarisation

7. Find the *Code of conduct* on the CMBA website and read it thoroughly.
8. Ask a friend, colleague or family member to assess your knowledge about the code. (You must be 100% confident that your actions in practice reflect the *Code of conduct*.)

2.4: Choosing a professional association

9. Investigate each professional association and compare their mission.

10. Find out what their activities entail (ie. how they spend the premium that you pay them), research their fees and ask colleagues about their experience.
11. Table your findings, rate the answers and choose the one that has the most advantages for you.

2.5: *Cover the basics – keep your first aid qualifications up to date*

12. Check your first aid certificate and determine the date of expiry.
13. Find a first aid training course in your area.
14. Mark the date in your calendar and book your course.

2.6: *Life story and timelines*

15. Make yourself available for 45 minutes.
16. Sit down in a place where you feel comfortable and relaxed.
17. Take a piece of paper and start putting down all the activities you have undertaken throughout your life.
18. Think about each individual situation and write down what you learnt from it.
19. Incorporate all you have learnt into a short story about yourself.

2.7: *Effective consultations*

20. Have a friend, family member or colleague take the role of a patient who comes for an initial consultation.
21. Role-play the consultation from arrival until farewell.
22. Make sure you know the structure of your consultation well, and try and stick to the times you have assigned for each activity during the session.

This activity is a non-academic activity, so there is no need to make it look good or presentable. It's a way to tap into what you want to bring into your clinical practice.

2.8:   *Create your self-care plan now*

Answer the following questions and, from your answers, write a plan for how you will take care of yourself personally and professionally.

23. In the past, when I felt unwell, what treatment modalities worked for me?
24. In the past, when I felt unwell, what did I do to make myself feel better?
25. Who is the first person that I am going to tell when I feel unwell?
26. How much time do I realistically need to allow myself to recover?
27. What are the immediate actions that I am going to take to ensure self-care?
28. Who is holding me accountable?

Congratulations, you are one step closer to success. For further worksheets and templates, go to www.brigittelinder. com.

ELEMENT 3: BRIDGE BUILDING

COLLABORATION AND MARKETING

"Let's build bridges, not walls."

—Martin Luther King

We will now talk about how you market yourself – Yes, that's right! – to create a message to attract patients to your business and assist you to describe your skills and how they can help your patients. Being smart and building bridges to reach your target market (or target patients) will help your business and clinic to blossom!

This is not limited to new patients, but to everyone who is going to be important in your new endeavour as a Chinese medicine practitioner. This is not just about marketing, but about encouraging you to engage with suppliers and your community while continuously building your profile. To collaborate is very easy; all it requires is talking to other people. But some of you may find it hard to talk about yourself and what you do. You love helping people in the treatment room, but you might find it difficult to actually 'sell' your services.

Megan Hills, Business Coach from Ethical Practice, has brought her expertise in marketing, graphic design and copywriting into this Element in the 'Marketing Made Easy' section. Megan has an outstanding set of skills and, from all I have seen and experienced, her approaches are nothing short of perfect. Marketing and branding don't need to cost an arm and a leg as long as you are well prepared and organised and have your essentials worked out.

BUILDING YOUR PROFILE

Rome wasn't built in a day and so your profile will take a little while to grow traction. What's crucial is that you maintain consistency. I have found that popularity and a good reputation are not built on being famous or on charging an exorbitant amount of money for your treatments or herbs, but on knowing how to connect with people on a simple and intrinsic level.

You have learnt great acupuncture skills and can prescribe outstanding Chinese herbal medicine formulas. Over and above that, you are a person who easily connects with people and explains things in clear, simple language. Despite the personable touch, you can rest assured that you will be a very popular practitioner if you remain professional.

As we live in a world where anything and everything can be researched or purchased 24/7 on the internet, it's important to educate your patient thoroughly and provide them with all appropriate options. It's also essential for retaining faithful and happy patients who will shout out about you. The better your skills are in explaining what you do, how you do it and what the expected outcome might be, the easier it is to take those patients on board and make them your new flag-bearers – people who find acupuncture and Chinese herbal medicine outstanding and recommend it to everyone.

Finding common ground

Patients tend to understand the language of the naturopath more easily because they are used to the terminology of Western medicine such as 'low iron', 'iron storage', 'thyroid hormones out of balance', 'liver readings through the roof' or 'kidney function impaired'.

Patients relate to those terms more easily than 'liver Yin deficiency', 'blood deficiency', 'qi stagnation', 'blood stasis' and so on. They have no idea what they mean and there is also the potential for them to imagine the wrong thing.

I wasn't really aware of this language problem when I first graduated. I felt proud that I had learnt all these things about human physiology and how all our microsystems connect holistically. Only when I started working with patients myself did I realise that instead of winning those patients over, I was alienating them as they had no idea what I was talking about.

As a practitioner, we act as an intermediary between the two worlds; we translate and bring our world closer to our patients. This is the best way to build our profile. It is an essential skill to be able to explain Chinese herbal medicine, acupuncture, cupping and moxibustion in our language but present it in a way that is easy for the layperson to understand. It has taken me a considerable amount of time to perfect this skill.

> As a practitioner, we act as an intermediary between the two worlds; we translate and bring our world closer to our patients.

I find that patients are fascinated by the Chinese medicine philosophy and, at the same time, they have a natural resonance with the explanations that I provide of how one body part or system closely relates to another body part or system. I always make 100% sure that my patients understand and follow everything I say to them. If they are confused, I pause for a moment and think about what may have caused a misunderstanding. I then try to clarify by using language or concepts that we are both familiar with. In this way, I bring the conversation back onto common ground and never leave my patient guessing about my intended meaning.

Respect and honesty

No matter what they come in for, patients will always ask for guidance regarding their diet, unless they simply don't want to change anything at all about their current food (and alcohol) intake. You will build your profile by being proactive and opening up those conversations. You will get a sense which patients are more than happy to comply with your recommendations and which would love to make changes but simply can't. It's great to respect just where your patients are at in life. It's not for us to judge our patients but to support them and work with them.

I encourage you to be honest with your patients if the treatment doesn't progress as expected. Sometimes acupuncture and Chinese herbal medicine are not the right modalities for an individual, even though you may have treated someone with a similar affliction successfully. It happens. Don't be disheartened by it but discuss other options with your patient. I can assure you that they are more likely to return to you or refer people to you if you are honest with them.

Developing communication skills

Communication skills are incredibly important when building your professional profile. If you have problems expressing yourself, you must spend time developing this skill. If you require a lot of time to explain what you mean, find it difficult to find the right words, or are unable to maintain eye contact or vary your tone, it might be time to look into improving your communication skills. You might want to join your local Toastmasters club or sign up for a professional communications workshop. You must become proficient and confident in communicating with your patients.

Building your profile will take a little time. There are many aspects to it, not just your ability to treat people. It is also about how you communicate, manage and follow up with your patients. Be consistent with your approach and only change an approach if you have outgrown it or if it isn't working. Remember, we are all finding our own rhythm and the best way to help our patients.

CONNECTING WITH YOUR COMMUNITY

Living in a small regional community has made it easy for me to connect with current and prospective patients. Not a single day passes when I don't run into my patients – sometimes in unusual places such as at a friend's house or at a party. I see them at the gym, the market, the shops, the dentist and the veterinary surgery – everywhere. I found this quite challenging at first because I am naturally a private person, but I now thoroughly enjoy living in a small community and connecting with people outside the treatment room as well. I have also found that the way I interact with individuals in my community provides me with a continuous flow of patients and referrals.

If you live or work in a suburb of a large city, you are still part of a small community. Like-minded people connect easily; it's simply a matter of finding them. When considering a prospective location for your practice, simply look up the local council/shire on the internet and find out what type of demographic lives there. This way you can prepare yourself well for your future patients.

Speak to people about what you do and how you do it

Connecting with your community – in a way that you feel most comfortable – is essential to the success of your business and your practice.

Demographic data is helpful to create your branding and your message to attract patients. For example, if there is a large proportion of retired couples who inhabit your area, you should target your potential patients with marketing collateral they will understand. In this case, there is no need to talk about problems with fertility, but rather look at menopausal conditions or problems of the renal system, diabetes and other conditions that affect people later in life.

What I have found works really well is to target some of the local clubs and find out if they need a guest speaker. I would then find out the profile of their members and tailor my topic around issues likely to affect them, obviously focusing on the benefits of acupuncture or Chinese herbal medicine. If you are speaking at women's organisation, you could talk about the sevenyear cycle of women and the various stages of age (ie. periods, babies and menopause) and connect that with possible pathologies. Or you talk about childbirth and target young families in your area. This is the way I grew my clinic in my area.

Find out what people do, where they work and what their hobbies are. What are their lifestyles, where do they shop, and how do they entertain themselves and their family? What are their primary interests and what are their problems? Learning these things will give you a good idea of your target market and you can better ready yourself to promote yourself and your business.

Make sure that you also connect with other health professionals in your area. I invited every practitioner in my area to the opening of my clinic: massage therapists, osteopaths, chiropractors, hypnotherapists, counsellors, psychologists and Bowen therapists. My invitation clearly outlined the services I was planning to offer to the community. Additionally, I noted that I was building a network of professionals that I wanted to refer to and so I invited them to bring in their business cards and flyers.

My experience is that most allied and alternative health care professionals are open to connect and collaborate. General practitioners (GPs) in my area, however, are not so willing. Luckily, we now have an integrative GP on our team who is happy to share our space and combine conventional medicine with Chinese medicine. The community loves our collaboration and it seems to be just what patients want.

ALIGNING YOURSELF WITH QUALITY SUPPLIERS

I consider suppliers to be business partners: someone to team up with, share notes with and build collaboration. After all, their business impacts yours and yours theirs. My business has a process in place that we call 'profiling of suppliers': we visit suppliers and look at their products and where are they sourced, what the company's philosophy is and how they treat their employees and their clients. We consider the services they offer and if their goals align with ours. We use a checklist to assess and profile companies who deliver their products and services to us.

Connect with partners who align with your vision, values and goals as this will ultimately benefit your path, your practice and your business. This is why it is important to think about the values

> Connect with partners who align with your vision, values and goals.

that align with your vision and goals. Sometimes, you are not in a position to make those choices yourself, but as a contractor in a multidisciplinary or Chinese medicine clinic, you can still voice your opinion on suppliers and organisations that support the wellbeing of the profession.

With a supplier that you feel 100% comfortable communicating with, you could have a chat with them about opportunities for collaboration. For instance, you could discuss the possibility of raising money together to help out somewhere. Could you campaign together to raise more awareness and educate more people? Is there anything that you could both do to help your respective businesses become more established, sustainable and profitable? You just might attract what you believe in!

MARKETING MADE EASY

BY MEGAN HILLS

As a student or graduate starting out, it is important to recognise that marketing is essential to the success of your practice and your business. If you think that renting a room from an established clinic who promises to do the marketing for you means marketing is not relevant to you, think again. If you are setting up an independent clinic on a busy road and think that signage will be enough, think again. If you think setting up a home clinic means your costs are low and that the practice will just build up organically through word of mouth, think again.

Why think again? Because I have seen many practitioners make these assumptions over the years and it is rare that they succeed without committing some time, energy and money to effective marketing. What's the first step to effective marketing? To embrace it – to be okay with marketing. Many Chinese medicine practitioners often associate marketing with 'snake oil salesman'. But it doesn't have to be that way. Marketing can have integrity and it can have soul.

Marketing is the building of bridges between you, your practice/clinic and potential clients. There is nothing bad about it. It simply requires that you stand out so prospective clients can find you easily. It also allows them to make an informed decision if they will come and see you for a consultation.

Here are seven easy tools to follow without being daunted by it:

1. Your message

2. Elevator pitch and talking to others

3. Branding and printed materials

4. Websites and SEO

5. Google Maps and business directories

6. eMarketing/eNews

7. Social media

You don't necessarily need all these tools. And these aren't the only tools available. But understanding how they work will make a big difference in getting the word out there, particularly if you understand how to make them work for your practice. Every Chinese medicine practice is different. Your marketing needs are different to those of the next Chinese medicine practitioner. Answering the key questions in these next sections will help you to work out which tools might be best for your practice. It will also help make your bridge look inviting to walk across...

In general, people who don't know you aren't really interested in you. While people may be fundamentally good, they are usually busy, stressed (to some degree) and somewhat self-absorbed. They don't care about your passion, your mission or your 'practice values'. They are interested in how you can solve their health problem. Marketing is about helping connect the person with the problem with you – the person with the solution – for a happy outcome. How you appear as a professional is also important. They need to be able to trust you enough to make contact. You want to give them a reason to feel a rapport with you and trust you before they have even met you. The key to communicating this is your marketing message.

Your message

Your core message is the foundation of your bridge. The following six questions will help you create a message that has meaning for your future client. This message will guide all your communications with your prospective clients on your website, your brochure, your eNews and more.

1. **What problem(s) do you solve?**

   As you are just starting out, you may not have a specialist area – in this case, give a scope of three key complaints, such as 'Anything from fertility to back pain to stre*ss*'. Example: fertility issues; back, neck and shoulder pain; stress, depression and anxiety.

   Note: If you are a registered practitioner, please refer to your government regulation authority regarding the legal use of words and phrases relating to conditions in your promotional material.

2. **For whom do you wish to solve this problem?**

   Listing a particular type of person doesn't mean you will necessarily repel all others. It just means that your messages will lean in this direction.

   Example: women; aged 25–40; living/working in 5km radius; middle-upper income; weekend warriors.

3. **How do you solve the problem?**

   In other words, what you do in your sessions that solves your ideal client's problem(s). Example: 'Amelia combines massage and acupuncture, creates a treatment plan, dispenses herbs and gives diet/lifestyle advice that is easy for patients to integrate into their lives.'

4. **What does a client experience?**

   In other words, what is having a session like with you? What happens?

Example: 'Amelia generally spends 5–10 minutes with the client, both sitting in chairs, talking through the issue. Then the client relaxes on the treatment table (fully clothed) for 35–40 minutes while Amelia applies very fine needles – how many depends on the issue. The final 5–10 minutes is spent discussing what happened in the session, what happens next (via a treatment plan created especially for the client) and how the client can best help themselves in between sessions.'

5. **What makes you special as a practitioner?**

Why should a prospective patient choose you over someone else who practises with the same or similar modality and/or specialises in the same area(s)? Imagine your ideal client and how they are most likely to describe what makes you special – this is likely to be about your personality and approach rather than your experience as a Chinese medicine practitioner.

Example: 'Amelia's clients often say that she is good at asking the right questions so they can both be clear on the right approach sooner.'

6. **How do people find you?**

In other words, what is the physical address (include any obvious landmarks), phone number, email and website (if one exists)? Can they get more information on the internet? Can they drop by to make an appointment? If you don't feel comfortable putting your whole address down, at least write the suburb.

Elevator pitch and talking to others

Have trouble talking with others about what you do? If so, you are not alone. While Chinese medicine has been around for hundreds of years – and has had a good stint in Western society over recent years – many people aren't aware of the value of Chinese medicine. So, when you talk about what you do you might find yourself educating people about your modality as much as about what makes you special as a practitioner.

An 'elevator pitch' or 'elevator description' is what you would say if, for example, you were talking to someone in an elevator about what you do. This other person asks what you do for a living and you have 15 seconds to give your spiel before the doors open and you've lost their attention. The aim is to be short and sweet but engaging.

So why write an elevator pitch and rehearse it? To make it sound natural. Sounds like a contradiction but rehearsing means you remember the important elements, so you can ad lib it in the conversation.

The answers to the questions you answered in the previous section will be the fodder for creating and delivering that clear message when you need to chitchat about yourself. Here are those questions again:

- What problem(s) do you solve?

- For whom do you wish to solve this problem?

- How do you solve the problem?

- What does a client experience?

- What makes you special as a practitioner?

- How do people find you?

Here is an example of an elevator description – with possible answers to the six marketing questions woven into it:

"Many of my clients have back and neck pain [#1]. They're often people who work at computers but also mothers and tradesmen [#2]. I have this special technique combining massage and acupuncture, but I also give easy stretching exercises [#3 & #5] that help my clients help themselves [#4]. My clinic is just up the road. You'll see the blue acupuncture sign near the intersection [#6]."

Being a newly graduated Chinese medicine practitioner means you may not have a special health condition focus. If this is the case, use a scope of two to three common conditions to give people an idea of the variety of different complaints treated. If you have a natural interest in a particular area then it may be worth considering promoting a niche, at least in conversation. For example, you could say, "I work with all kinds of conditions from back pain to fertility to digestive problems. I particularly enjoy helping people with stress and anxiety relief". What happens if the person you are talking to indicates that they could use your services? Just hand over your business card and say, "Call me anytime if you want to talk about it" – a gentle, easygoing way to end the conversation.

Branding and printed materials

In design terms, your brand is the 'look and feel' of your practice. It is not just your logo. It's how your practice looks and feels on your business card, signage, flyers, website, product labels, induction form, email signature, advertisements, etc. This 'look and feel' can also flow into the interior design approach of the clinic space.

Your brand must appeal to your ideal client *and* assist in communicating how you help them. Too often practitioners design their promotional material to suit their own taste. Your brand is not for you. It is for your ideal client. Yes, it helps that you like it. But remember that it is a bridge upon which they step to walk towards you.

It is also important to engage a professional to design your logo and develop your marketing materials. Many people try to design their own logo and business card – or have a friend or relative who is 'handy on the computer' do it for them. Big mistake. This is putting your practice on the back foot before it has even begun. Professional design and printing reflect your professionalism. Professionalism and trust work hand in hand. Amateur design means you see yourself as an amateur practitioner. So, then, the natural question from a prospective client is 'Why should I trust you with my health?'

Logo and tagline

A logo is a specific design used to identify your practice and informs the general branding approach of your practice. Your logo doesn't need to be a 'symbol'. It can be the way the letters of your practice name are designed using particular fonts and colours. It may also include a 'descriptor' – your practice name may be 'Evolve Clinic' but underneath your practice name your descriptor may state 'Acupuncture, Massage & Chinese Herbs'.

Think of your logo as a two-second experience. If a stranger looked at your logo for two seconds, what impression would they get? Is it attractive? Is it informative? Make sure your logo is simple and uncluttered, original (because what you do is special), communicates something important about your service that will appeal to your ideal client and is practical in how it will be applied (ie. it will work well on your business card, website, uniforms, car signage, etc).

Taglines, also known as 'slogans', are short phrases that communicate something emotive about your practice. They are designed to emotionally inspire action by your ideal client.

A tagline example is 'Fertility focus with gentle care'. Taglines appear in your branding, but not necessarily your logo. Taglines aren't compulsory, but they are helpful if your practice name and descriptor don't say quite enough or inspire enough.

Business card

In the world of electronic media, the humble business card still has a powerful place. Chinese medicine clinics exist in communities. People in those communities still like to look at your card, keep it in their wallet or take it to pass onto another person. First impressions count. And your business card could be that first impression. Someone might pick it up from another clinic, a café or health food shop. This means your card needs to effectively communicate on your behalf. What does it need to communicate? How you can help and what makes you special.

First impressions count.

Have a look at the components that make up a professional business card:

- logo

- tagline (optional)

- your name/title

- phone number (bold)

- address

- email

- website (if you don't have a website yet, buy a profile in a well-ranked online health directory and have your URL link to that until you are ready to have a proper website)

- academic qualifications (after your name)

- association memberships and registration credentials

- social media icons.

Tip: make sure all these details are on the front of the card as flipping the card to get the key information is annoying.

You can use the space on the back of your business card to write next appointment dates and times. You can also repeat your logo and phone number so it is easy for the client to refer to. But this is up to you. If you wish, you can include incentives on your business card to help to inspire contact, such as:

- cost saving: 'Health rebates may apply'

- fast-track booking: 'Easy online booking' (include URL)

- creating a relationship: 'Free eBook with online subscription to eNews'.

Branding brief

In order to have a logo and business card designed professionally, it is best to create a branding brief to assist in quoting the job and to guide the designer who wins the job. It is also worth asking for a business card design and email signature design at the same time (this puts your logo/branding in useful context).

The brief should include:

- practice name/descriptor

- tagline (if you have one)

- core services (preferably top three in order of importance)

- what is special about this practice

- description of your ideal client

- existing Chinese medicine practitioners who are similar to you in your area

- keywords to describe how you want to appear (to be appealing to your ideal client) (eg. friendly, trustworthy, professional, calm, sophisticated, corporate, natural/ organic, contemporary)

- any recommended colours (and why they will be appealing to your ideal client)

- anything to be avoided (specific symbols, colours, etc.)

- how your logo will be used (eg. business card, website, flyers, health directories, clinic signage, car signage, uniform)

- business card content.

Signage

Whether it's affixed to your clinic building, on a sandwich board or on your car, make sure your signage is simple with strong branding continuity. Look at the design for two seconds and consider what information is gleaned. Light colours on a dark background are *much* easier to read at a glance than the reverse. Your modality and website address can be more important than your clinic name and phone number. You still need your clinic name there as a logo, but phone numbers are being overtaken by website addresses for quick searching (make sure you have a touch-to-call phone number on your website header). If you have a sandwich board outside the clinic, do not waste valuable space by putting the word 'OPEN' on it, as its location outside your clinic already indicates that you are open.

Brochures and flyers

A general brochure can be useful, folding to DL envelope size to fit into racks. But also consider having a series of DL flyers. On the front of each flyer focus on a specific health complaint and how you approach it. Perhaps include some useful tips, if appropriate. Flyers should have a catchy headline at the top and an attractive photograph to draw the eye. On the back of each flyer is your standard clinic information, perhaps with a photo of you and your clinic room. You can buy some single DL stands and distribute them with a mix of your flyers through local cafes, health food stores and any outlet that will accept them which your ideal client might visit. This need not be expensive with online printers. Or support a local printer if you can afford it – they might promote you in return. Again, hire a designer to create the artwork, ensuring your professional profile has a consistent, professional and attractive brand.

Websites and SEO

We are getting to the point where practitioners look less than committed if they don't have their own website. New practitioners should certainly have their own website as they don't have a large referral base to rely upon that more experienced practitioners are likely to have. Do you plan to work (or are working) in an established multi-practitioner clinic? Does that clinic have a well-ranked website with a page dedicated to you? If so, that's a good start. But you still may be hard to find on Google and that could be the undoing of your practice. Even if the clinic's website is well-ranked, it doesn't mean that you are.

Your bio on a multi-practitioner site

If you are renting a room in a clinic, then the clinic probably has a website and you have a photo with a paragraph or two about your service. If your profile is on the same page as other practitioners, it might be worth discussing the option to have a click-through to a page dedicated to you and your modality, so you will be easier to find on Google. But if sharing a page with others is the deal, then it is a matter of making the most of it.

Some guidelines to an effective practitioner bio include:

- photograph – head & shoulders, clear, professional, friendly

- qualifications, memberships and modalities (list after your name)

- social media link(s) with icon

- bio text – write from the clients' perspective and remember the six key marketing questions. For example, instead of 'I feel passionate about this and that' your bio could state: 'If you have [list of ailments] then I [explain what's special about your approach] which has the benefit of [explain what you are working towards but without promising success]'.

These details are also helpful when setting up the 'About' page on your website.

Writing for the web

Have you ever gone to a website to see a huge essay with a sea of words that just keeps going? Off-putting, isn't it? I call this the 'Dead Sea scroll effect'.

If you would like to have a go at writing your own web content, here are some tips:

- Use short sentences.

- Break text up in short, bite-sized paragraphs led by a subheading in bold.

- Use bullets for short lists (don't overuse bullet points – long bulleted lists are hard to read).

- Use a conversational tone (ie. not too dry)

- Write from the client's perspective (ie. 'What's in it for me?') Avoid things like 'our mission'. No one cares – they want to know how you can solve their problem.

- Use keywords but don't overdo it (more on this soon).

- Insert calls to action (eg. 'Book here').

If you are going to hire someone to develop your website, then write a brief for them to quote on – and be guided by if they get the job. What is in a website brief? It may include:

- practice description

- ideal client description

- pages you would like

- technical features, such as social media links, sign up to eNews, contact form, Google Maps and online booking

- words to describe the feeling you are after (eg. contemporary, professional, caring, fresh, simple/clean, calm, corporate, natural/organic, elegant)

- existing websites that illustrate style or functionality you would like to incorporate

- what content already exists, such as text, graphics and photos

- what content still needs development and who is likely to do this.

Images on the web

Time and time again we see the same – or similar – photos to promote natural therapies: a pile of smooth stones, a lotus flower, a single drop in clear water, acupuncture needles in an apple or pretty-looking raw Chinese herbs. They're everywhere, right? Admittedly, hiring a professional photographer can be expensive, so photo libraries can be useful. The problem is that Chinese medicine practitioners are all starting to look the same. And that's not good. We want to let your future ideal clients know how special *you* are. Think about the pages on your website and what images might need to go on each. Again, keep in mind what will be most helpful to your ideal client.

Here are some kick-off suggestions:

- you talking with a client

- you demonstrating exercises

- you discussing different herbs with a client

- attractive design details of your practice (if the calming space is part of the attraction)

- your treatment room

- street view of the clinic.

Repetition of images in other promotional materials is a good thing. It can help reinforcement of your 'brand' (your 'look and feel'). Hiring a photographer? Then create a list of what photos you think you will need and where they are likely to be used. Wherever possible, use natural light. Be conscious of what time of day your clinic is best lit. Also wear clothing that is simple and, where possible, reflects your brand. Photographers often forget about the need to crop an image to fit a format (eg. the main image on your website homepage under the menu), so request space for cropping for all images.

SEO and keywords

Search Engine Optimisation, otherwise known as SEO or Google ranking, is a book in itself. But we can address the basics. Much of your Google ranking is dependent on keywords. If you are an acupuncturist in Sydney and someone types the keywords 'Acupuncture Sydney' into the Google search field, you would hope they see your practice high up on the first page.

For helpful Google ranking, you need good keywords and phrases in the following three areas:

- modality ('acupuncture' is more popular than 'Chinese medicine')

- geographic area (suburb, surrounding suburbs, city, state)

- health complaints specific to your area (be careful how you insert conditions in your material – abide by the guidelines given by your government registration body).

The goal in SEO is to be as high as possible on the Google list of certain words and phrases that your ideal client is likely to use in order to find you.

To increase your chances of Google rewarding you with a higher ranking, keywords and phrases should appear in the title of your pages, in headings and subheadings used, and in your body text – but only if it reads naturally. Google penalises keywords that don't appear in a logical, useful manner to the visitor. It is equally important to ensure that keywords are inserted in the meta tags of each page. Meta tags are snippets of text that describe a page's content. They only appear in the code of your page and not on the page itself. Discuss meta tags with your website developer to ensure you have your bases covered there.

The more pages you have on your site with specific words and phrases, the better (ie. the less competition you will have from other sites). For example, 'pain' is fine but many practitioners have 'pain' on their websites, so the competition to be on the first page of Google for 'acupuncture Sydney pain' is high. 'Back pain' has slightly less competition while 'lower back pain' has less competition still.

Google Maps and business directories

Sign up for a free Business Profile on Google My Business to ensure you are listed on Google Maps. When searching 'acupuncture Sydney' via Google a map of Sydney will appear at the top (or top right) of the page showing the top Google Maps listings for that search. Under the map and associated listings are the general search results. For these general results, beyond the Google Maps listings, there may appear links to specific clinics. However, some may be links to clinic listings on online business directories. It is recommended to take a listing on these directories as a way to take advantage of their page on Google ranking.

eMarketing/eNews

Even if you decide not to have a website at first, you can still keep in touch with clients and prospects electronically with a newsletter. You can have eNews sign-ups on Facebook and on certain online health directories (contact them to find out if this is possible). Setting up, creating and sending out a regular eNews is relatively user-friendly using an email marketing platform like Mailchimp* and is free up to a certain number of subscribers and posts. There are other eMarketing platforms out there that might suit you better. It's best to post monthly, bimonthly or quarterly. Don't overdo it, for your sake and theirs.

Note: I do not receive any commission or incentive from Mailchimp for mentioning this product. It's just what I use.

Having legal permission to remind people you are still around is a powerful and beautiful thing. You will have clients who will drift off from time to time. They mean to book in again for a session, but they get distracted. Until they receive your eNews. The perfect generous, non-invasive prompt to say 'Hey, I'm still here for you – no pressure'. Or a current client may forward your eNews article to a friend and that friend might book with you. Or they may post it on their social media pages – spreading their love of what you do to all their contacts.

Your eNews content can consist of an article. But if writing is not your thing, consider publishing a short video or podcast (audio file) that addresses a specific but reasonably common health problem. Remember that any articles, videos and podcasts on your eNews can also be posted on your website and social media.

Here are a few tips for your eNews:

- Make sure your template has branding continuity in terms of your logo and colours.

- Have a catchy headline.

- Give practical, easy tips.

- Write short sentences/paragraphs/bulleted or numbered lists with subheadings to encourage the reader to read on.

- End with a call-to-action – 'Read more...', 'Click to download...', Call me...', 'Book here...'

- Have an unsubscribe link at the end.

- Provide a freebie in exchange for signing up.

Ensure you have permission to send your eNews to someone (via paper agreement and signature on your clinic intake form or via opt-in boxes on your website, links from social media, etc.) otherwise it is considered spam. Don't pass on your list to someone else to use as this is breaking privacy laws, and don't forget that an unsubscribe link must be available in all your eNews publications/campaigns.

It is becoming increasingly rare for a person to subscribe to another's email list without receiving something immediately valuable in return. For your sake, it's best to make that free gift an automated download of something digital. It could be a small eBook, a podcast or a video series. Promote that freebie with an attractive visual of some kind. A thumbnail image of the cover of the eBook (or akin to this) is helpful so they can see what they are going to receive – and this builds further trust and enthusiasm. Also consider having an eNews sign up section on your new client intake form. If you do this, you must ensure it is clear your new client is giving you legal permission to email them your eNews campaigns.

Social media

Facebook has had a good track record of being the world's most popular social media platform. Unsurprisingly, Facebook is the most useful social media platform for most health practitioners to connect with their ideal client as it is so popular.

Other globally popular social media platforms include LinkedIn (useful for developing relationships with other practitioners to foster referrals), Google My Business (Google+ which is helpful for being found on Google Maps comes under this) and YouTube (owned by Google so helpful for ranking).

You might enjoy using Twitter or Instagram but do your prospective clients? This leads us to...

Who do you connect with? What do you post?

Get in the shoes of your prospective clients and join them on social media platforms that they already engage in – not just the ones you are comfortable with. Consider connecting with the 'community' of your ideal client (eg. local businesses and schools), health networks and those relevant to your specialty. Be careful mixing personal with business. For example, your personal politics might not be the same as some of your likers and you can lose valuable followers fast by spouting opinions carelessly. And remember, people are busy, so keep posts brief. But, where appropriate, link to your website for more information.

What kind of content should you post? It is worth mixing it up to keep your profile interesting to others. Posting a video or your latest eNews article shows you are an expert in your field (with a link back to your website for the full article). Sometimes one well-written sentence can be powerful. Inspirational quotes that resonate can still earn some serious traction. Sharing other people's content is a good idea too – as long as it is relevant and appealing to your ideal client. Google Alerts makes finding relevant content recently posted on the web easy to source.

What is a good social media strategy? Try for scheduling one post per day. And consider splitting your content into three groups:

1. One-third dedicated to content about your practice – this could be your eNews articles, short videos, podcasts, information about clinic services, new products for sale, etc.

2. One-third dedicated to an image with a quote. These are so powerful on social media and it's great if you can put your website address discretely at the bottom of the image that has the quote on it.

3. One-third dedicated to sharing something helpful from elsewhere.

Facebook Insights and advertising

Facebook Insights helps you to understand the visitors to your page (by age, gender, location and when they are online) and which posts are being received well and which aren't. With this information, you can adapt your marketing to enhance the impact (and reduce the time you need to spend on this!) Facebook advertising is an incredibly effective and cheap way to be able to build your business page exposure and increase your likers. You can set your budget, target audience and end dates. It need not be expensive and, if set up right, can be very powerful.

The power of repetition in marketing is never to be underestimated.

The power of repetition in marketing is never to be underestimated. A person generally needs to see your marketing material (in whatever form) on average *six times* before considering taking action. But this also means being active in the community (both offline and online) and being patient. It also means assessing what content is most popular and how you can shift your messages to ones that might have more meaning to your ideal client. Marketing can be an experimental process of testing and altering and testing again. None of this marketing activity is worthwhile if your service doesn't reflect the professionalism of your marketing. In other words, you must walk your talk.

ELEMENTAL SELF-CARE

Does promoting yourself feel challenging? Remember that marketing is simply telling our prospects what we do to help solve their problems. Clear communication is needed as well as consistency and persistence. We tend to give up too early and stop the good stuff before it has had time to sink in.

We all receive so many messages every day about things that we 'need' and should buy or have. But in order for the message to be clear to us we need to hear and see it multiple times. Be consistent and clear in your approach. It's a good quality to embrace in business and will serve you well in life too. Be brave, be clear and be consistent!

ELEMENT 3 ACTIVITIES

These important exercises will inspire you to embrace marketing activities and brush up on your communication skills. Set aside ample time to complete these activities.

3.1: How effective are my communications skills?

This activity is an honest self-assessment of your current communication skills. Answer the following questions truthfully or, if that's difficult, talk to a trusted friend or colleague and ask them to help you answer the questions.

1. How much time do I spend explaining myself?
2. How easily do I come up with simple explanations of complex topics?
3. Do I often get a sense that other people have no idea what I am trying to tell them?
4. Is it easy for me to maintain good eye contact?
5. Can I easily demonstrate a varied vocabulary tailored to my audience?
6. Can I present my ideas easily, clearly and concisely?

3.2: What are some of the values that I look for in a partner/supplier?

Your answers to the following five questions will ascertain the qualities and values that you are seeking in a partner, supplier or wholesaler. Collaboration is effortless with like-minded businesses.

7. I only want to work with suppliers who are...
8. I expect them to have the following terms and conditions:...
9. Have I met them personally and what is my impression?
10. Do they support our industry and how?
11. In which areas can we work together?

3.3: Write your elevator pitch

You have 15 seconds to tell someone who you are and what you do. Answering these six questions will help you create an interesting, concise speech with a natural flow.

12. What problem(s) do you solve?
13. For whom do you wish to solve this problem?
14. How do you solve the problem?
15. What does a client experience?
16. What makes you special as a practitioner?
17. How do people find you?

3.4: Brainstorm your business name and tagline

Your business name and brand are about communicating what you do and how you solve the problem(s) of your ideal client.

18. List some succinct and easy to pronounce/spell business names that reflect the essence of how your practice helps others. Consider if it would appeal to your ideal client, taking into account their problem(s).
19. Does your preferred business name reflect what you do? Or do you need a descriptor underneath to clarify it? If so, write the descriptor.
20. Find out if your preferred business name is available to register and if you can buy the website address for it.
21. Write a short tagline (try four words maximum) reflecting an important emotion or action relating to what you do and how you help others.
22. What symbols have been overused in Chinese medicine? Why would it be good to avoid these?
23. If you were to have a symbol as part of your logo, what would it be? Would it be helpful and/or inspirational to your ideal client? What does it say to them?
24. Is there anything specific about your location that would make you easier to find?

25. Ask people you know who have nothing to do with Chinese medicine but reflect your ideal client if your business name and descriptor (and tagline and/or symbol if you have one) are clear and attractive enough to inspire a call to make an appointment.

3.5: Draft the contents of your new business card

Here is an opportunity to be creative but, once again, concise. Your business card has to be handed to someone with pride not with excuses. So make it a good one.

26. Does your name clearly stand out?
27. Are your qualifications listed?
28. Are all contact details clearly identifiable?
29. Is your website there?
30. If you have a logo, is it integrating nicely with the rest of the text?
31. Is your brilliant tagline clearly visible?
32. Do you use the backside of the card to write your appointments down?

Congratulations, you are getting the message out. For further worksheets and templates, go to www.brigittelinder.com.

ELEMENT 4: SYSTEMS

PRACTICAL TOOLS
AND TECHNIQUES

"For every minute spent organising, an hour is earned."

—Benjamin Franklin

Being organised is being in control. You are about to commence your business venture (whether you are contracting or running your own show) and you need to be organised in numerous aspects. If you are entering employment in a paid position, you still need to be organised especially in the treatment room. Joining another business also means that you will have to bring your best game to the table.

> Being organised is being in control.

I assume you love doing treatments as that must be one of the main reasons why you studied Chinese medicine in the first place. But your business is not only about treating and talking to people; it's also about structures, tools and the systems around it. Other tasks such as ordering stock, keeping patient files up to date, keeping CPD records, bookkeeping, paying bills, and keeping an eye on your income and expenditure can easily take the wind out of your sails. Be prepared and it will be a breeze.

This Element explores the tools and systems that work well in the Chinese medicine practice setting. Believe me when I say that to be organised and have systems in place is going to save you from spending the wrong resources at the worst time. Being organised in your clinic and business is part of how you plan for success.

Developing a rhythm or flow is what provides you with consistency and allows for completing tasks and achieving goals. You spent some time in Element 1 exploring your goals (both short-term and long-term). You also investigated and captured values that resonate with you and, by now, you should have developed a fair idea on where you are heading. If you are still unsure, please go back to Element 1 to work out where you want to be in ten years' time. If you are unfamiliar with your chosen path, spend more time investigating and exploring it.

ORGANISATIONAL TOOLS

Organisational tools are a means to help you remain focused and be effective as a business professional. Not planning and not being organised is one of the weaknesses in our profession. We might accomplish a lot with our patients and be great at applying our skills in the treatment room, but who does this serve if our business venture doesn't survive? Be organised with basic tools and you will create success for yourself.

I hope to inspire you with tools that will help you stay on track to achieving your goals. For most people, writing down your plans is easiest and most effective, however if you are an auditory person, take advantage of technology and record your plans.

Kanban: visualise your work projects

Kanban is a great visual tool originally used for a production system to improve workflow. The word Kanban originates from Japanese and translates to 'signboard' or 'billboard'. Toyota still uses the Kanban system (originally introduced by Taiichi Ohno, an industrial engineer) to improve their manufacturing efficiency. The closest English word that reflects the meaning of Kanban is 'queue limiter'.[14]

From the grand vision and bigger picture you have created, you now need to bring steps and tasks into the present and, most importantly, make them visible. Kanban boards are great for this. In my business, we use Kanban boards to help put ideas down, then prioritise, implement and complete them. Adopting the Kanban system has allowed us more clarity and better collaboration across teams as our practitioners also work with the team at the dispensary.

The two major advantages of using a Kanban board are that it's visual and the tasks in the 'Doing' column are limited to three, which encourages focus and reduces multitasking and overwhelm. We have one board in the clinic and one in the dispensary and each team member has a different colour.

The Kanban boards we use in my business are laid out in the following way:

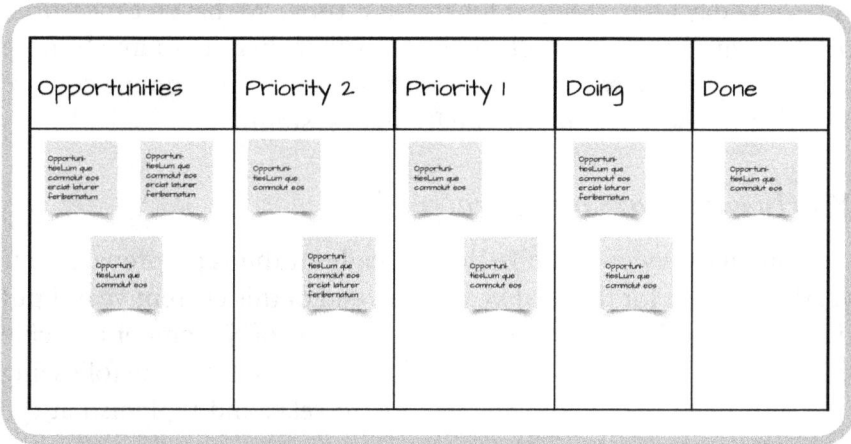

Opportunities	Priority 2	Priority 1	Doing	Done

There are three simple rules to the Kanban system:

1. Visualise the work – improved comprehension, faster recognition.

2. Limit the work in progress – single focus, higher efficiency.

3. Maximise throughput (ie. output) – faster response, quicker feedback.

Instead of writing lists of things to do, we use one sticky note per task with all tasks classified as opportunities (rather than 'things to do'). If there is a deadline associated with that task, we will add the date. We allow only three sticky notes per person in the 'Doing' column. We keep them there until the task is complete or we put it into one of the priority columns if we require external input.

We also move sticky notes from the 'Opportunities' column with its large number of tasks into the 'Priority 1' or 'Priority 2' column to represent what is actually happening. The Kanban is more a flow system than a static things-to-do list and everyone loves moving the sticky notes around the board. The most satisfying action is moving a sticky note from 'Doing' to 'Done'. It's so liberating.

So, the first system you could adopt in your own business is the Kanban board. It made so much sense that we implemented it the very next day after seeing it for the first time. We haven't measured productivity yet, but my observation is that there is so much more clarity, it's fun *and* we are getting stuff done. There are online courses available to learn how to use the Kanban system.

Yearly calendar: an overview

To gain an overview of activities throughout the year, prepare your yearly calendar for the next year at the end of this current year. I put time aside (perhaps four hours) in the middle of November to tackle this task. It helps me to know exactly what I am doing the following year and I can then allow myself time to relax and replenish at the end of the year.

The type of items I schedule in my yearly calendar are:

- conferences and seminars I want to attend

- five or six clinic events

- newsletters and marketing campaigns

- advertorial deadlines

- monthly webinars that I run

- meetings and training with my team

- weekly mentorship sessions with the other practitioners

- monthly blogs for both the dispensary and the clinic

- my time off, including long weekends and holidays.

By having everything planned out from the start of the year, you will keep yourself accountable for attending to these tasks. It will also help you coordinate with everyone else – other practitioners, industry partners, suppliers and allied health professionals – who you are working with in your business.

Default diary: planning week to week

Another system I have recently adopted is the default diary. I plan and time important activities at specific times throughout the week or the month. Default means that if something happens by default, it happens only because someone does not do something else. This someone is *you*. And *you* are blocking time in your weekly and monthly diary so that you won't be doing anything else at that allocated time.

Yes, it might sound uninspiring but, as creatures of habit, planning important activities helps us stay focused. By using a default diary, I know that I can make it through my week and actually get things done. I also appreciate that all the activities I need and want to do have a place in my diary, including my dog walks, training classes, critical thinking sessions, finance reviews, advertorial writing and quiet time.

On my clinic days, I no longer try to accomplish a long list of other tasks such as paying my car registration, making an appointment to see the dentist or talking to my accountant because I keep to what I have planned in my diary. For example, on the three days that I consult with patients, I treat patients, write referrals, look at research, read through patient files and follow up with patients. This keeps me in the clinic zone and I can use my energy simply for that. As I start early and finish late on my clinic days, I make sure that I am in the right mindset when starting my day. These three blocks are well marked in my diary as clinic shifts so that I don't do other things unrelated to this work.

When starting out, you tend to book patients in at a time that suits them best. Regardless of whether you are working as a contractor, in an employed situation or as a sole trader, I encourage you to have clinic shifts (as many as you want) marked out in your diary and take appointments during those times only. Outside of these times you can attend to activities associated with running your business.

I also suggest you mark on your diary when you are going to take time off for self-care. I take myself out of clinic 1 week in every 12. That is what I personally need to recharge. It's time away from patients to concentrate on projects requiring big blocks of time. It doesn't mean that I go on holiday (although it can if I need it); it is simply catching up on studying, reading, planning or writing. I will not see any patients for the whole week.

I understand that this might not be financially viable when starting out. But remember that at the start of your practice there are a lot of other things to be accomplished besides treating patients. There are a lot of decisions to be made and time is required to reach a good decision. My business coach recommends allocating four hours each week to work *on* the business – planning, reading, learning, reflecting, improving – rather than *in* the business. During this time you should focus on making your business run better or train yourself in business skills.

When planning your weekly diary you will need to consider:

- your regular activities or appointments

- which days to set aside for seeing patients

- the length of time required for each task

- which day could be your troubleshooting day to attend to small but necessary tasks

- putting aside time to think critically, assess, reflect and work on your business.

You need to be realistic about how much you can accomplish in a short amount of time. Be aware of not overloading your weekly diary; you will want snippets of time to honour what you have achieved.

> You need to be realistic about how much you can accomplish in a short amount of time.

Your checklists

Produce a weekly checklist for weekly recurring tasks. Do the same for monthly, quarterly, semi-annually and yearly tasks. You can use Kanban items (sticky notes in the 'Doing' section) to help you produce a particular checklist. For example, you might have a sticky note on your Kanban board to find new premises to accommodate your clinic space. The first item on your checklist could therefore be 'create a list of features for the space', followed by 'determine location', 'create a budget', 'look up RealEstate.com', 'contact agents' and so on. If there are not too many items, create one list with the various timelines: weekly, monthly, quarterly, semi-annually, yearly.

Here is an example of items that need to be on a checklist:

- mentoring sessions (weekly)

- advertorial for local newspapers (monthly)

- BAS statement (quarterly)

- superannuation payment (quarterly)

- continuing professional development portfolio (yearly).

Accountability

In recent years, I have found that I can decide or plan anything I want but if I am not accountable, it will never happen. How do you hold yourself accountable? You have to be willing to answer for the outcomes of your choices, actions and behaviours, and accept responsibility. When you are personally accountable, you stop assigning blame and making excuses. Find yourself an accountability buddy who will hold you accountable.

As Jan L. Bowen states in her article 'How Accountability Leads to Success', "Accountability doesn't guarantee that you always get the result you want. It means that you've acted in integrity with your choices and actions, and can stand behind them because they are congruent with what is important to you".[15]

PRESCRIBING AND DISPENSING HERBS

In Australia, Chinese medicine practitioners traditionally maintained their own herbal dispensary. Herbs found their way into the country when the first Chinese settlers arrived, attracted by the gold rush in Victoria in the mid-1800s. While it's a long-standing and commendable tradition, the expectations of the public have changed. During your undergraduate course, you would have worked in your university's herbal dispensary since it's an integral part of the profession. Herbal dispensing is a registration category and it requires specific training and expertise. Furthermore, the CMBA *Guidelines for safe Chinese herbal medicine practice* (discussed in Element 2) has come into effect and must be adhered to.

Should I do my own herbal dispensing?

When I speak to students, they always tell me that they want to have their own herbal dispensary. As a herbalist, this is a natural desire, and I had it too when graduating. The reality is that it requires a lot of time and attention to run your own dispensary.

A few years ago, I decided to ask other practitioners about their herbal dispensing practice. At the time, over 60% of practitioners I spoke to felt that herbal dispensing was problematic for various reasons. The most important issue for them was access to quality herbs. The second issue for practitioners was the resources required to build and maintain a complete herbal dispensary. Time, effort and cost are often underestimated when it comes to professional herbal dispensing, especially if you decide to run solo. Herbs do expire and some raw herbs have a shorter lifespan than others. Some herbs are used more than others but the less common ones might still be needed. Stock management must take all of this into consideration.

If you are just starting out, I don't recommend building up your dispensary as a top priority as you will need your resources (both time and money) for consulting with patients and promoting yourself and your business. You should ensure that you are comfortable with your time management in the clinic room before thinking about running your own herbal dispensary.

Before seriously considering setting up a herbal dispensary, consider the following questions:

- Is the space available?

- Is there environmental control (heating or cooling)?

- Which herbal form are you intending to stock and dispense?

- Where are you going to order stock from?

- Have you put money aside to pay for stock?

- How are you going to manage your stock?

- How will you keep track of expiry dates?

- What type of storage containers will you use?

- What type of labels will you use?

- How will you keep your dispensary clean?

- How do you ensure that a repeat prescription is exactly the same as the original?

- How will you double-check your dispensed formulas?

- Do you have some type of batch management system in place?

From my own experience and consultation with many practitioners over the past ten years, I believe that a herbal dispensary is worthwhile running if there are several herbalists in a clinic sharing the dispensary or when you have developed into an established practitioner with a high number of patients per week, by which time you would need help with dispensing in order to keep consulting at the same level.

Forms of herbs

In Australia, we are spoilt for choice as countless types of herbs and herbal products are available. The following information will help you to choose the right products and suppliers for your practice.

Raw herbs and powders:

Powders are raw herbs that have been ground and are not otherwise processed, except by traditional processing methods such as steaming, honey frying, dry frying, etc. Using raw herbs is still the preferred way to prescribe herbs for practitioners, because all our textbooks are based on their qi, their effect and movement in the body, their dosage and their processing. In recent years, however, patients have become less keen on cooking raw herbs, which has brought about processed forms of herbs such as liquid extracts and granules.

Liquid extracts:

In my clinic, I work mostly with liquid extracts as they are the most popular form of herbs and are very high in compliance. Liquid extracts are easily taken by children and sensitive individuals. Their processing is similar to granules (concentrated) but they undergo a slightly different manufacturing process. All liquid extracts come from traditional sources in China. The manufacturing of liquid extracts involves two steps: cold maceration and distillation.

Maceration is achieved by soaking raw materials (herbs, minerals and some animal parts) in a combination of alcohol and water for various amounts of time depending on the part of the plant. Leaves and flowers are macerated for a shorter amount of time than roots, branches and minerals. If used after maceration, they would be called tinctures and contain approximately 45% alcohol. But liquid extracts are now distilled, the second part of the manufacturing process, so that the alcohol is removed from the product.

The production of liquid extracts differs to traditional water extracts in that alcohol dissolves a greater number of constituents in the herbal substance than water alone does. To make the liquid extracts stable for an extended period of time, they are preserved with glycerine. All liquid extracts have the same concentration ratio of 5:1 which means that they are five times stronger than the same amount of raw herbs.

Granulated extracts:

Granulated extracts are available both as single substances and as pre-packaged formulas. All pre-packaged formulas must be listed on the ARTG. Granules are made by boiling raw herbs in pressurised vats to extract the liquid, which is then sprayed onto a carrier. Some manufacturers use the starch of the herb being processed, while others use corn starch or potato starch.

Each herb has individual properties and, depending on various factors relating to the region or the harvest time, each batch can have a different concentration ratio, which is often adjusted with the plant starch to ensure consistency. Some manufacturers produce a ratio of 1:5 (meaning 1gm of granulated herb is equivalent to 5gm of raw herb), while others produce ratios of 1:6 to 1:8. Other manufacturers produce clearly defined ratios of 1:5, 1:10 and 1:20. The higher the concentration, the more questionable the extracts are, as there is only a certain amount of extraction possible in natural products.

Choosing quality products

You must be 100% confident that the products you ask your patients to take are reliable and sourced ethically. It has become common for patients to question the source of products they are recommended or prescribed. The resources section has a list of suppliers that can provide you with quality herbs and other products.

Patent formulas (Cheng Yao), more properly referred to as 'proprietary medicines' or 'manufactured medicines', are pre-packaged formulas available off-the-shelf in the form of tablets, pills, powders or capsules. In Australia, all therapeutic products must be manufactured according to GMP pharmaceutical standards and must be listed or registered on the ARTG by the sponsor of the goods. A sponsor, according to the TGA, is a person or company that imports, exports or manufactures therapeutic goods (or arranges another party to import, export or manufacture therapeutic goods). The listing and registration of therapeutic products on the ARTG attracts an initial registration fee as well as yearly fees.

Products that a Chinese medicine practitioner recommends or prescribes are likely to be listed (rather than registered) on the ARTG. Sponsors who list a product are not permitted to make any therapeutic claims about the product because there is no scientific evidence to sustain that claim. In comparison, a registered product can claim therapeutic effects because it has undergone testing to prove the claim. Formulas or products that are labelled with an AUST L number have been listed on the ARTG and are deemed to be good quality, with the safety and quality of the ingredients having been assessed by the TGA. Listed products are often sold commercially over the counter without requiring a consultation with a registered Chinese medicine practitioner.

In comparison, the use of single herbs, particularly granules, that are dispensed or extemporaneously compounded by practitioners may not be required to be included on the ARTG. In this case, you can be assured of a quality product that comes with a Certificate of Analysis (CoA) from a GMP manufacturer. This is the type of product to offer to your patients. With a certificate in hand, you know that you have the right botanical identity, that it has been tested for harmful substances and that heavy metal levels have been measured. Furthermore, you will know that it is free from bacteria. You can't go wrong with a single herb that comes from a GMP facility. A limited range of raw herbs are available that are accompanied by a CoA.

Giving products to patients at your clinic

The best thing about using herbal medicines is that you are able to give your patient their medicine at the end of their consultation, no matter if you are handing them patents (ready-made medicines) or a formula that you have just dispensed for them.

You must consider the possibility of a patient having an allergic or other reaction to one of the herbs in a formula given to them. That's why it's important to take your time with your prescriptions. The more detail the better is a general rule that I apply to my prescriptions.

How to label herbal products

Labelling requirements are not only for the information of the patient but also provide information to other health practitioners who might share their care.

The CMBA *Guidelines for safe Chinese herbal medicine practice* state that the label of any herbal medicines given to a patient must be written in English with individual herbs listed in either Pinyin or the scientific nomenclature.

Other details to be included on the label are:

- patient name

- dispensing date

- individual ingredients and dosage

- dispenser name and contact number

- specific directions and cautions

- warnings where relevant.

The guidelines also state that the label may be a copy of the prescription providing that all information is included.

For raw herbs, the main label can be on the outer pack, with the inner packs bearing at least the name of the patient and the dispensing date. The preparation instructions are to be in English or in the patient's own language. It is acceptable to have the cooking instructions on a separate sheet of paper or they can be part of the labelling.

Manufactured herbal medicines (patents) are to be supplied in their original packaging showing an AUST L or AUST R number, which means that the product has been listed or registered with the ARTG. These products come packaged and labelled with a standard dosage indication already printed on the box or bottle. A practitioner can modify the dosage if need be, but the original label must not be obscured.

It is also important to note that practitioners who are registered in the division of acupuncture only can dispense patents but if they customise herbal formulas for patients, they are obliged to disclose to their patients that they are not registered to do so. If you are prescribing manufactured herbal medicines (patents with an AUST L or AUST R number), similar rules apply.

Prescribing herbal medicines only

If you are prescribing a herbal formula for your patient to take to a third-party dispensary, you need to follow the basic guidelines even more carefully, particularly in regard to:

- the name of the patient

- your own contact details and registration number

- your signature

- individual dosage for each ingredient

- the number of packets (where relevant)

- the date prescribed plus the expiry date of the prescription

- repeats (if any)

- clear directions for preparation and administration

- the form of processing

- specific warnings where relevant (eg. take two hours away from Western medication).

If you have more than one patient from the same family, it is a good idea to identify each pack of herbs to avoid the risk of another member of the family taking the wrong pack.

The same rules and instructions apply to herbal extracts, but the preparation instructions will be different. If the total amount is supplied in a single container there is no need to state the number of packs or write separate labels for each pack. For easier handling you can also dispense doses into daily sachets.

A third-party dispensary is fully equipped and licensed to meet the GMP standards, which are much higher than those required of practitioners. Furthermore, a dispensary can backtrack each ingredient to its source as all ingredients of any herbal formula come from a GMP supplier. Each prescription prepared by a GMP licensed dispensary will bear the batch number of each herb in the formula which allows them to recall medicines immediately in the event of an emergency.

Advise patients about potential adverse effects

Always makes sure that you advise your patients about potential adverse effects. Encourage them to contact you if they have any concerns about any part of the treatment. Establish a protocol in your clinic to handle any complaints and be aware of your reporting responsibilities should an unexpected reaction occur. All formulas prescribed or dispensed need to be noted in the patient's health records. For the retention of those records, you must comply with the requirements of the State that you are working in.

In a nutshell, if you are clear that you will be dispensing your own herbs, no matter what form, be clear on how you will manage your herbal dispensing. The *Guidelines for safe Chinese herbal medicine practice* highlights the potential for conflict of interest when self-dispensing. You must ensure that when prescribing and supplying a medicine for your patient that it is in the patient's best interest, not yours.

If I prescribe a herbal formula that causes unexpected effects such as diarrhoea, stomach pains or vomiting (this can often be because the herbs have an unusual taste and the patient can't actually stomach them), I will review the dosage and ask the patient to call again in three days. If it's still impossible for them to take the herbs, I might offer them a modified version. Depending on the situation, I may make the replacement formula complimentary, especially if it's the first time the patient has taken Chinese herbs. I am the first to admit that our prescriptions are not always perfect, no matter how much time and effort we take to make them up. And with new patients, we sometimes just can't anticipate how they might react to herbs physically.

As I do with acupuncture, I explain extensively to patients how Chinese herbal medicines work so they understand that the herbs will support their system and stimulate proper physiological function. I also explain that the composition of the herbal formula might change along the way (for seasonal and cyclical reasons) and that they will not have to take them indefinitely.

Restricted herbs

Chinese herbs listed in the *SUSMP* have certain prohibitions. Scheduling is a national classification system that controls how medicines and poisons are made available to the public. Medicines and poisons are classified into Schedules according to the level of risk they pose.

Schedule 1 (S1)	Not currently in use (but is a potential schedule for Chinese herbs Zhi Fu Zi and Ma Huang)
Schedule 2 (S2)	Pharmacy Medicine
Schedule 3 (S3)	Pharmacist Only Medicine
Schedule 4 (S4)	Prescription Only Medicine / Prescription Animal Remedy
Schedule 5 (S5)	Caution
Schedule 6 (S6)	Poison
Schedule 7 (S7)	Dangerous Poison
Schedule 8 (S8)	Controlled Drug
Schedule 9 (S9)	Prohibited Substance
Schedule 10 (S10)	Substances of such danger to health as to warrant prohibition of sale, supply and use

Some herbs important to Chinese medicine practice have been included in Schedules 2 and 4 because of their toxicity. This includes the aconite species (Fu Zi, Zhi Fu Zi, Wu Tou, Cao Wu and Zhi Cao Wu). The ephedra species (Ma Huang and Ma Huang Gen) are also included in Schedule 4 and both plants carry additional restrictions in the relevant schedule. Huo Ma Ren (Cannabis seeds) is in Schedule 9, which are poisons that are considered drugs of abuse; the manufacture, possession, sale or use of these are prohibited by law except for amounts which may be necessary for educational, experimental or research purposes.

This means that as Chinese medicine practitioners we don't have access to some important herbs which have no satisfactory substitutes that can be used safely in line with our protocols for preparation, administration and dosage. While there are justified concerns with toxicity levels in Wu Tou and Cao Wu, and with raw Fu Zi, the herb Zhi Fu Zi is safe for use when properly prepared and providing dosage protocols are followed. Similarly, Ma Huang is safe for use when following traditional dosage and administration protocols. Other herbs, however, such as Guang Fang Ji, Ma Dou Ling, Guan Mu Tong and Xi Xin are understandably prohibited because they contain carcinogenic aristolochic acids.

In view of those considerations, the CMBA is currently supporting the profession's proposal to have Ma Huang and Zhi Fu Zi rescheduled as Schedule 1 substances. The submission demonstrates that we are knowledgeable in the use of those herbs and can handle those substances safely. At the time of writing, this submission has been accepted and we now await an update on the status of the proposal. Keep an eye on the CMBA's website or newsletter for updates.

Pharmaceutical standards for complementary medicine

GMP is a worldwide standard for the manufacture of therapeutic goods and medical devices. It applies to pharmaceuticals, medicines, tools that are used, materials that are implanted, blood products and substances used in complementary medicine. GMP is based on protocols (standard operating procedures) that define each and every step for preparing medicines. The focus is on making each preparation consistent and, above all, safe.

It's a whole new ball game and, thankfully, Chinese medicine practitioners are exempt from having to comply with the code. The reason for this is the personal communication between patient and practitioner and the customised preparation for that particular patient. If you supply herbal products to a person other than your own patient, the medicines must be manufactured or otherwise compounded according to GMP.

Although following the correct guidelines to administer a product to your patient can be quite complex, the objective is to ensure that every product, whether consumed internally or applied topically, is of the highest quality and the most appropriate for the patient. Chinese herbs and acupuncture cannot be dismissed as being ineffective, however they can carry risk if used incorrectly, if there is human error or if there is an idiosyncratic adverse response.

As responsible registered health professionals, we do ourselves an injustice if we do not acknowledge those facts. It is irresponsible to believe or to claim that our treatments are 'safe and effective'. Even if most of our treatments are safe and effective, and even though 'safe and effective' is the mantra driving regulation criteria, such a generalised statement tends to mislead the consumer.

Our wise acknowledgement of the potential risk of some treatments and some herbal substances is crucial to our reputation as a responsible profession that is capable of managing those risks and, importantly, qualified to use, dispense and prescribe such herbs as Zhi Fu Zi and Ma Huang that are so valuable to our practice and remain without satisfactory substitutes.

ADMINISTRATION SYSTEMS

The patient management system is central to your business. It doesn't matter if you use the traditional paper trail or if you embrace an electronic solution; either way, how you administer patient information is essential and it has to be spot on.

> The patient management system is central to your business.

At Safflower clinic, we have created a paper and an electronic (online) version of the initial consultation form for both adults and children. It's a combination of open-ended and multiple-choice questions. This form also contains a 'Consent to receive treatment' section that they must initial and date. For their follow-up consultation, I use a shorter and simpler version.

I am able to create and modify these forms easily and quickly in Cliniko, my current practice management system.

Patient records

Until recently, I used a paper-based record system, but have recently transitioned to online patient records that are part of Cliniko. As patient records contain sensitive data and Cliniko is cloud-based, extra security measurements have been employed such as industry relevant certification standards, encryption and two-factor authentication.

If patients bring in reports from medical investigations, I can scan and attach them to their Cliniko record. A copy of their herbal prescription is also added either as an email attachment or copied across from the online ordering system that I use with our dispensary. In this way, all important information is found in one place in chronological order.

If a patient asks for their record, it can be printed out immediately. Bear in mind at all times that they have the right to so. This is an extra bonus of using an online system. I highly recommend using a practice management system as they also integrate with other areas of patient management, not just patient records. As you know, our patient records need to meet the standards of the CMBA – visit the CMBA website and simply search for 'code and guidelines' for full details.

You will find a number of useful articles on the internet comparing various practice management systems so use this as a starting point and do your research as to which system is the best fit for you and your business. Important considerations include pricing, platform (cloud-based or onsite), claims, online booking, integrations with accounting and other software, ability to send SMS and email notifications to patients, secure messaging, invoicing, data backup and support.[16]

Referral templates

Many patients come in with complicated conditions and are also seeing other allied health practitioners. One of the reasons my clinic has such a good reputation is that I make sure I work in collaboration with other disciplines.

I have created template letters to use in such situations, so when another practitioner refers someone to my clinic, I send them a letter or email thanking them for the referral. This will include how many sessions we have planned for the treatment of the condition and how we are going to approach it. Once that treatment prescription is completed, I report back with the status. At that time, I might also refer the patient back to the original practitioner. In this way, I keep a professional relationship with other health practitioners and the patient doesn't have to report back themselves to each practitioner involved.

Following up appointments

We follow up each initial appointment in two ways. First, we send a general email to thank the patient for choosing our clinic and at the same time remind them of potential adverse effects of the treatment. This reminds them that some of the sensations they might experience are completely normal. It also provides them with an opportunity to call if they are concerned about their body's response or if the herbal medicines are causing diarrhoea, abdominal pain or nausea. In turn, it will give us an opportunity to clarify details or take action if needed.

The second method that we use is to send a personal text message to the patient to inquire how they feel. It shows that we care and encourages them to check in with their body. It also serves to remind them of any discussion we may have had about diet or lifestyle changes.

Appointment reminders

All our appointments are sent an automatic text message reminder the day before their scheduled time. Needless to say, it is vital to have appointment times booked at optimal levels.

Cancellation policy

Late cancellations and no-shows are part of patient rapport as you will have to deal with them if you don't have a receptionist. It's annoying and upsetting if a patient cancels 30 minutes before their scheduled appointment or, worse, doesn't come at all and when you ring them you find they have completely forgotten about it.

It took me a while to create and enforce a cancellation policy. My clinic now has the following rule in place: When patients have not presented at the clinic by ten minutes into their appointment time, I ring them. If they are running late, depending on how late they arrive, I might still do a shorter treatment, but still charge for an entire session. If they cancel late, we point out that we would prefer 24 hours' notice because we have a cancellation list and someone else might have been able to take their spot with sufficient notice. The first time this happens with a patient I am lenient and do not charge a cancellation fee, however if it happens again, I charge them 50% of the consultation cost.

Occasionally, you will get patients who are persistently late or hit you with last-minute cancellations frequently. Perhaps a reminder that it's part of their responsibility to show up for their booked appointments could help.

We have copies of our cancellation policy in the waiting area, on the initial form (both paper and online), on the 'Next appointment' card, as part of the booking and reminder email, and with each text message reminder that is sent automatically one day prior to the appointment. If we take a booking on the telephone, we state the policy verbally as well. Since implementing this policy, patients take more responsibility for giving us plenty of notice for cancellations or rescheduling appointments and we have received fewer complaints about having to pay for missed appointments.

Discounting treatments

In the past, I have had patients who were under financial pressure and found it hard to pay the full price for treatments. That extra challenge in their life often adds to an already significant amount of stress. In order to make affordable services available to everyone, we opened a community acupuncture space in 2017 where we offer low-cost treatments in a multi-bed setting.

Bookkeeping

Bookkeeping refers mainly to the record-keeping aspect of accounting. As a business owner, you are responsible for recording all the information regarding the transactions and financial activities of your business. You can find useful information on setting up a bookkeeping system in the Finance/Accounting section at www. business.gov.au, an online government resource for the Australian business community.

PRACTICAL TECHNIQUES AND TOOLS TO KEEP YOU ON TRACK

The theory about treating patients is just one aspect of our profession. You will find that the practicalities vary greatly. Over the years, I have encountered many uncomfortable situations with patients because I was unprepared for them, and I now understand that learning how to manage those situations was an important part of my development. Patient rapport is very much the driving force of your interaction with the patient. I have found it to be a key ingredient of the treatment outcome as well.

As a new graduate, there are many challenges outside patient interactions. Unless you have a team that includes such personnel as a receptionist, a bookkeeper, a marketing or branding manager, a dispenser and a cleaner, it's pretty much all up to you. It could also take a little time to get into a good routine with patients.

Active listening

One of the first skills you must master is active listening. It requires you to fully concentrate, understand, respond to patients appropriately and then remember everything that was said. I take a fair number of notes when listening to patients which has two advantages: the patients get the message that what they say is really important and it helps us to remember their full story, including any subtle mood changes.

> One of the first skills you must master is active listening.

It's not difficult to develop active listening skills. There are three simple steps involved:

1. Pay attention (to what your patient says).

2. Demonstrate you are listening (receptive body language, nodding or saying yes or no).

3. Provide feedback (that is relevant to what your patient said).[17]

I also encourage you to practise your active listening skills every day in every situation that you encounter – at your local shop, with your neighbours, your friends, your family and any other communication that you are part of – so that it becomes a natural part of who you are.

Utilise the five elements

Understanding the Worsley Five-Element Acupuncture model provided me with ground-breaking insights into how people behave based on their element type.[18] Learning about the five element types of personalities was incredibly helpful in my daily interaction with patients. For example, in the past, I had difficulties dealing with assertive patients (because they can be demanding), but I then learnt that the wood-type patient (who is demanding, assertive and often critical) likes to have their energy met, so in that situation I now simply imitate and mirror the wood-type personality. I encourage you to look into five element acupuncture courses to become familiar with its principles to help you manage difficult patients more effectively.

Another way is to take an interest in the psychology of people. What drives them? What makes them talk the way they do? Why are they being difficult? Just like the concept popularised by Joe South's song 'Walk a mile in my shoes', I strive to adhere to the adage 'Before you criticise a man, walk a mile in his shoes'.

Your body language and receptivity

Body language, which includes our facial expressions, body postures and gestures, forms our non-verbal communication. Our breathing conveys clues to our mood or state and is part of our physical expression as well. We tend to read body language instinctively and receive clues from it.

Whenever you interact with a patient, but particularly the first time, pay close attention to their body language. At the same time, monitor your own non-verbal expressions as your thoughts express through kinetics. I find that if I simply sit and receive what the patient tells me, my body language remains neutral, relaxed and receptive.

I take notes of what patients say and elicit more information with gentle questions. I keep them on track. I simply hold the space to provide them with an opportunity to freely express. If they divert, I will bring them back to the point we were talking about. I allow some digressions if I believe the additional information is important in providing a more complete picture that would permit me to give them a better treatment.

Once the patient feels more comfortable with me, I might become a little more animated or even make a joke if appropriate. I always tread very carefully though; never overstep the line by engaging in idle gossip or expressing a strong opinion. With patients I have treated for a long time, I might have a conversation about their family or about a local incident, but I make sure I never cross the line and always keep it at a professional level.

I tend to maintain eye contact throughout the conversation. The eyes are the windows of the soul and we connect deeply by looking into each other's eyes. I keep my gaze soft as I look into my patient's eyes and only if I observe that they are uncomfortable with this will I avert my eyes and then usually mirror what they do.

Language

If a patient comes for their first consultation and they have never explored acupuncture or Chinese medicine before, be careful to explain everything in simple terms. If a patient shows great interest and is keen to venture deeper into Chinese medicine concepts, you can expand into more complex theory. I find that most patients do not understand Yin and Yang, zang-fu theory or the five elements. To make sure they understand, I will ask them: "Do you understand what I mean?" and "Do you understand how this applies to you?"

> Explain everything in simple terms.

You can read in their face if they truly understand or if they are just saying they do to make you happy.

The language that I use might, for instance, give them an explanation of kidney deficiency. I explain in simple words what that means exactly and relate it to their current situation. We have all experienced – and will continue to experience – how patients ask for a herb for this problem or a substance for that problem. This is where Chinese medicine differs from other modalities. I make sure the patient understands that Chinese medicine works by treating the whole person and not one part or one symptom. I continue to clarify with them that by gathering all the information that contributes to their problem we will be able to identify and treat their pattern. The purpose of Chinese medicine is, in fact, to identify and to eliminate or transform the root cause of health problems. This is exactly what patients want and they are relieved to hear that is what we are attempting to achieve through treatment with Chinese medicine.

Guidelines for physical contact

Each time you come into physical contact with a patient, be conscious that you are entering their personal sphere. If you shake your patient's hand when they first come in for a consultation, make sure it's not too firm or too loose. The handshake is a welcome greeting and should make patients feel that they are in good hands.

Physical touch is associated with investigating a patient's problem and also includes pulse-taking. Various methods of pulse-taking exist, but it is *how* you touch that matters. Whenever I touch, I will use all my concentration to make it a respectful but gentle gesture that is confident, reassuring and caring.

In my clinic, I use abdominal palpation, especially for digestive or reproductive disorders, or to clarify the choice for a particular herbal formula. I explain the physical palpation beforehand and I always ask for permission to touch. I make sure that my hands are warm and that the genital area is covered with an extra towel to give an added sense of privacy. Then I palpate the abdominal area and note my findings.

Other types of palpation might be used to identify the channel implicated in pain or discomfort. I often check the temperature of the feet and hands. Sometimes I feel the skin on the lower legs or, in the case of lower back pain, the lower back, to see if there is dryness, dampness, fluid accumulation or other things going on.

Although you are likely to have your own methods for diagnosis, the important thing is to practise and be mindful of the way you touch patients.

Seek consent before applying a treatment

When you have finished your examination, you will prepare your patient for treatment. Even though they have signed a consent form beforehand, I suggest that you still ask their permission each time prior to inserting needles, particularly at the first appointment.

Before inserting the first needle, check once again that the patient understands that there are potential side effects, such as feeling tired, feeling relaxed, feeling sensations on points used during the treatment that can be felt for some time later, bruising and, in the worst-case scenario, pneumothorax.

If a patient is frightened of needles they will feel anxious, so it's important to take extra care when conducting the treatment.

Treatment plan and referrals

In all these years of practising and going to appointments myself, I have learnt that instructions must be in writing. Patients only partially remember the consultation. They can also be overwhelmed with so much new information and foreign concepts. In my clinic, I use a 'Treatment Plan' form where I note down the findings, recommendations and further notes.

If you discuss a referral with your patient, write a professional referral letter to the chosen health practitioner. It's up to you to show your professional manners when working with allied health professionals or medical practitioners. Prepare a referral template that you can modify quickly when needed as this will save you a lot of time.

Dress code

Looking professional in the clinic setting is an added factor in being successful. One of my patients dresses up whenever she goes to a specialist appointment as she's convinced they treat her much better. Do clothes make people? Yes, they do... even though they don't.

What is professional dress attire? The perception of professional clothing varies from individual to individual, however in most industries, it means wearing a suit, a dress, trousers or a skirt and button-up shirt with matching jacket in neutral colours such as grey, navy, brown and black. If you feel completely uncomfortable in clothing like this, you may tone it down a bit. But do remember that being professional comes with certain obligations including dressing appropriately when consulting with patients. Professional attire projects professionalism.

I have work clothes and I have casual clothes. I choose simple styles in various colours that I can easily combine. I also keep one or two pairs of shoes at work that I change into. My 'work shoes' are comfortable, easily coordinate with my clothes and have rubber soles, which allow me to move quietly on the wooden floors of the clinic.

Consistency is the key

These are some of my most important tips for you. Following these tools and techniques has allowed me to build a great rapport with my patients and a reputation that keeps a flow of new patients coming to the clinic. The fact that my patients trust me to refer them to other practitioners (when required) tells me that my aim of creating a space of trust and confidence is working.

Once you have found a rhythm that gets you into a flow, keep it steady for at least six months rather than frantically changing things every day. Most things on this planet, business ventures included, take time. To build a base or expertise in something, including running a business injected with your essence, requires patience and persistence. Constant dripping wears away the stone, creating an impression. The flow evolves from what you know and what comes from you so keep it simple at the beginning.

If you are working in someone else's business, make sure that some kind of framework – a way of doing things – is in place. It helps greatly in gaining consistency. Steadiness extends to the team and creates a great environment. Meet the team to ascertain if the business is consistent and steady, and ask yourself if a position is going to be conducive to the way you want to practise.

> Having systems in place before you start is essential.

When working for yourself, whether at home or in commercial premises, having systems in place before you start is essential. A simple framework provides you with stability, and consistency will then flow through all areas of your practice, no matter if you are in the creation phase or if you have been at it for a while. All things take time, but they might take a shorter time if you are consistent in your approach.

ELEMENTAL SELF-CARE

As Leonardo da Vinci said, "Simplicity is the ultimate sophistication". When things (or cases) become too complicated, I use simplicity to see it through. You are in control and can apply a simple approach, a simple attitude or a simple gesture at all times.

This is a simple reminder to keep things simple and go back to the basics so that ultimately you can flourish. This is key for practitioners to remember while juggling treatments, building patient rapport, income concerns, bookkeeping, professional development and keeping up with regulations and trends.

ELEMENT 4 ACTIVITIES

This Element has discussed individual systems and tools that will make life easier for you on a daily basis. The following activities are particularly important to help you be organised and productive at all times. Please take ample time to complete them.

4.1: Create your yearly activity calendar

1. Start thinking about some of the activities you want to offer in your business.
2. Research event dates that are important for you and that you need to plan around (eg. CPD, conferences, retreats, family events, weddings and birthdays).
3. Choose your preferred media to schedule all those events, preferably on one piece of paper, one Excel spreadsheet or one electronic calendar (I have an online and a paper version).
4. Put those event dates into your preferred calendar. Be as committed and concise as you can.

4.2: Plan your weekly diary

1. What regular activities or appointments do you currently have?
2. Which days do you dedicate to seeing patients?
3. What are the tasks that need bigger chunks of time?
4. Which day could be your troubleshooting day to carry out small tasks that need to be accomplished but are usually quick and easy to do?
5. What time will you allocate to think critically, assess and reflect? Put aside at least four hours per week to work on your business.

4.3: Create your checklists

1. Define all your weekly tasks and write them down.
2. Define all your monthly tasks and write them down.

3. Define all your quarterly tasks and write them down.
4. Define all your half-yearly tasks and write them down.
5. Define all your yearly tasks and write them down.

4.4: Role-play active listening in your consultation

1. Choose a friend or colleague who you trust.
2. Choose some basic sentences and words that you are going to use.
3. Role-play your initial consultation with them using the problem of hay fever.
4. Ask your friend or colleague to give you feedback and recommendations.

The more you practise, the better you will become and the easier your language and communication with your patients will flow.

4.5: If you are going to work for yourself, determine how you can achieve consistency

1. I have identified tools to keep me on track and remind me of my goals.
2. I have found an accountability buddy to make sure that I do what I say I will.
3. I am conforming to all CMBA guidelines.
4. I am applying a system for the use of herbs that I can manage easily.
5. I know how to report potential adverse effects to the TGA.
6. I am familiar with the herbs currently restricted in Australia.
7. I am comfortable talking to my patients.
8. I am comfortable touching patients.
9. I am confident that my patient records are spot on.
10. I am happy with my choice of practice management system.
11. I am clear on what my financial responsibilities are.

Congratulations! If you have come this far, you are well and truly on your way to being super organised. Rather than making your life hard, the tools and techniques covered in this chapter will help you remain focused, effective and on track to achieve your goals and success. You may be great in the treatment room and accomplish a lot with your patients, but who does this serve if your business venture doesn't survive? Be organised with basic tools and you will create success for yourself.

For further worksheets and templates, go to www. brigittelinder.com.

ELEMENT 5: REVIEW

REFLECTION AND REVISION

"Sometimes, you have to look back in order to
understand the things that lie ahead."

—Yvonne Woon

As you gain more experience and expertise in growing your business and dealing with patients and their concerns, you should aim to integrate that learning into optimisation of yourself, your interaction with others and your business itself. This Element is about playing an active role in the cycle and encourages you to review what you do on a regular basis. I see this as a semi-annual or yearly process.

As part of our yearly review in the dispensary at Safflower, we conduct a self-inspection. This helps us to deal constructively with mistakes and remain consistent and effective in the production and compounding of medicines. This chapter introduces the Plan-Do-Check-Act (PDCA) quality management system that can help to iron out any deficiencies or ineffective practices.

Those who have gone before us are best placed to teach us what they have learnt from their mistakes and their successes, and so I am pleased to present you with interviews with a number of experienced and highly regarded Chinese medicine practitioners. Their stories will provide you with encouragement and inspiration to grow, develop and never stop learning. They talk honestly about both their successes and mistakes in order to help you to avoid pitfalls and overcome obstacles.

LEARNING FROM AND DEALING WITH MISTAKES

We are human and are not perfect; we are bound to make mistakes in our daily life, work, interactions and even in reflection. But the good thing is that most mistakes can be corrected simply by doing the same thing in a different way.

Surpassing my own and other people's expectations is one of the goals I set for my clinic. I also share this goal with other practitioners in the team and encourage them to find better ways of doing things, ultimately aiming for perfecting everything that we do. It is part of human nature to become complacent or lazy when we have done the same thing for an extended period of time. In a team, it's less likely to occur as we can keep each other in check.

> Your business and the way you operate is an expression of who you are.

To me, statistics are important, but I also associate excellence with a feeling or an internal mood that I experience. The combination of excellent clinic figures and feeling a sense of flow tells me that I am being successful. It feels like moment, occasion and outcome align. Throughout this book, I have tried to point out the importance of self and your vision, values and goals, because your business and the way you operate is an expression of who you are.

To thrive as individual practitioners and as a profession overall, we must embrace excellence. In this case, all our eggs need to be in the same basket! If we make a mistake, we need to take that seriously. In my opinion, we need to fix the mistake but should also reflect on the mistake in order to avoid it happening again in the future.

There are opportunities available every day to show that we are excellent, not only in our methods and modalities but also as human beings. An excellent profession is unbeatable, solid and

We must embrace excellence.

resilient. If we are excellent as individuals how can we not thrive as an industry? The desire to be excellent comes from within, but it reaches far and wide and has a tremendous impact not only on our own lives but on the lives of our patients and anyone that we are in contact with. It will go far beyond our current situation and impact on the next generation of practitioners as well.

PLAN-DO-CHECK-ACT (PDCA) QUALITY MANAGEMENT SYSTEM

In striving for excellence in your practice, a good quality management system is essential. One of the easiest quality management systems to follow is the Plan-Do-Check-Act (PDCA) method. It is also known as the Deming wheel after its inventor, Dr W. Edwards Deming. Known as a system for developing critical thinking, PDCA is a planned sequence that aims at improving a process or a product through systematic and documented activities.[19] You could regard it as a method of business management.

The PDCA system is designed to create consistency and improvement across all areas in your practice and business. The quality cycle of PDCA helps you to stay on track and ensures that your activities are monitored, whether that be treating patients, managing numbers, ordering stock, liaising with allied health professionals or even making your own products.

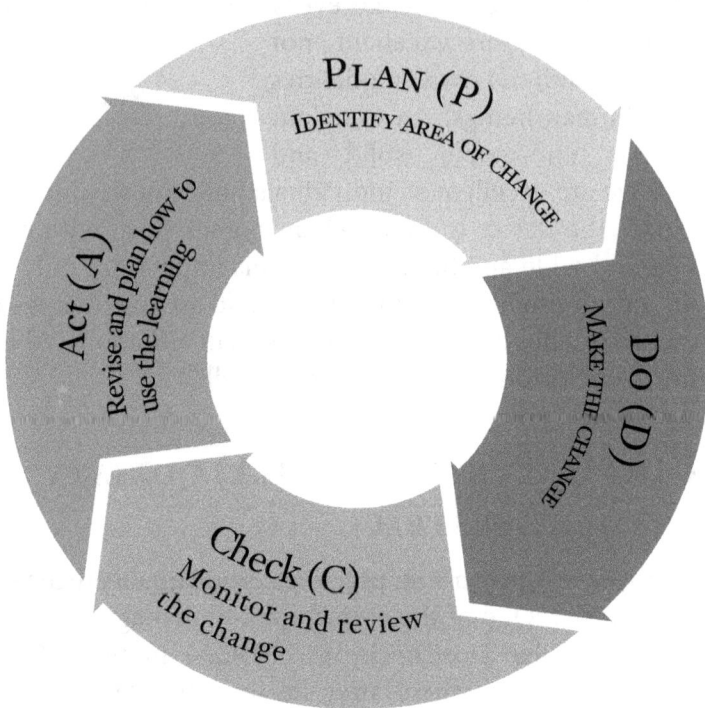

PDCA can be seen as one framework within a bigger one. It is more closely related to how you *do* things rather than how you *feel* about them. It doesn't take feelings and visions into consideration, but it is a great method to gauge your progress qualitatively and measure the outcomes of your efforts quantitatively.

The PDCA steps

1. Plan (P) – Identify area of change

During the planning phase, you will look at what needs to change or the factors that make you realise something needs changing. You would then look at the current process and interpret all information relating to it. This gathering of information should be extensive and involve patients, suppliers and anyone else who plays a part in your business. Next, you will identify opportunities for improvement and possible solutions, and document the objectives of the outcomes you would like to see.

2. Do (D) – Make the change

Now carry out the change and document the implementation activities.

3. Check (C) – Monitor and review the change

You will now monitor the progress of the implementation in accordance with your plan and evaluate its effectiveness. Document your observations and results, and compare it with the original situation to decide whether the implementation is successful. What did you achieve with the implementation of the change? Are the outcomes as expected? Checking should be continuous throughout the whole improvement cycle. It is something new, so you must keep an eye on it.

4. Act (A) – Revise and plan how to use the learning

Once you are clear on what you have learnt, what will you do with it now? Will you adopt or abandon the change or run it through another PDCA cycle? This is the last step but can also initiate a further review.

A practical example for your practice:

You might find this a little theoretical, so here is an example of how you could apply the PDCA cycle in your practice. You can put any process through the PDCA cycle.

Plan:

You decide to look at the way you respond to telephone queries about your business. What are the frequently asked questions and what are your answers? And how do these answers impact your business? What changes do you think you could make in the way you answer the phone? What outcome would you like to see from any changes made? You come up with a plan to use scripted responses to the standard telephone queries with an aim to improve your conversion rate and new patient confidence.

Do:

You will now implement your plan to use prepared answers to answer telephone queries. For example, if asked about the price for a consultation, instead of simply saying it costs $95, you use a scripted response to also say that the initial consultation is very important as it includes taking a full medical history and working out a management treatment plan. This immediately shows the value of the $95 investment which the potential patient is more likely to focus rather than only thinking of the $95 cost.

Check:

Chart your new patient numbers over the course of one week and one month to determine if this simple change has brought more prospects to your clinic. Monitor whether it has created better-educated patients – perhaps you are spending less time explaining the consultation process in the consultation itself.

Act:

Having determined that there has been an increase in your booking conversion rate (from telephone queries) and new patient confidence in the initial consultation you decide to implement this change. You decide to expand your scripted responses to include a wider range of queries.

In learning from this experience, consider other areas in your business that could benefit from a change in order to streamline the way you work and create more impact.

GEMS OF WISDOM FROM EXPERIENCED PRACTITIONERS

As a new graduate, there is so much you can learn from established practitioners and you should take every opportunity to do so. In this section, a number of experienced practitioners share their wisdom with you through a series of questions. This is a small sample of successful practitioners in Australia who have worked out a system that provides them with a continuous flow of new patients and a substantial disposable income.

The Chinese medicine profession is affected by high attrition rates, which means that many highly talented practitioners leave the industry within five years of graduating. Through this book, I hope to contribute to our profession and help lower attrition rates by sharing my knowledge in order to provide a better and more conducive environment for graduates to commence their practice. The more confident that practitioners at all levels of experience are with their practice and their business skills, the more patients we can help and the more our industry flourishes.

Clare Pyers
In practice since 2001, Discover Chinese Medicine (Richmond, VIC)
www.discovertcm.com.au

How do you determine success in your own clinic?

Success to me is more of a feeling than anything that is measurable. A big part of it is that I get enjoyment out of my clinic and that I don't feel like I am inhibited by the logistics of my clinic or worry about whether I have enough patients or enough money to pay bills. I get a good six-figure income by working just three days a week with patients and a fourth day from home on a little bit of administration.

I have also mentored a lot of other practitioners who have worked at my clinic and are now successful practitioners themselves. Through doing this, I feel like I am helping other people to be successful as well. Of course, to me, good patient outcomes are connected with earning a good living.

When you first started out, what did you do well and what should you have done differently?

The best decision I made when I started out was to introduce electronic patient records straight away. I only realise now how clever that decision was.

In terms of something I did poorly or would do differently, I was probably too eager to be liked by my patients, so I wasn't having difficult conversations with them when needed. This made it harder to get good outcomes for some difficult patients and being less effective also affected my patient rapport.

What is most important to you in your practice today?

The most important thing for me is that I love it; I love my clinic, the team and my patients.

What do you think can be done to improve the Chinese medicine profession?

In terms of education, there needs to be much better support for students relating to business education and all aspects of setting up a clinic. It's not enough to deliver one unit on accounting. Business preparation for practitioners is really poor which stops a lot of people from succeeding.

I would also like to see more successful clinics hiring practitioners; generally, there is a need for more jobs in our industry.

There is a real poverty mentality that prevails our entire profession. I would like to see more abundance. Compared to other industries, we have so much awesome stuff, but I still hear practitioners complain about seminars or the membership of professional associations being too expensive. It floors me that there are so many complaints about things like this – if people out there are not able to access us, there will be a lot of practitioners sitting around in empty clinics.

> Never settle for mediocre outcomes.

What important tip would you give to a graduate just starting out?

Don't undertreat your patients and never settle for mediocre outcomes. Our medicine works well and quickly. Change your treatment approach if there are no signs of improvement.

What other advice would you give to new graduates?

I advise all the students who come to my clinic to start planning long before they open their doors. They need to look at their pricing and value. Many practitioners undercharge. We provide a valuable service and need to charge accordingly. Offer each patient a full treatment plan and don't judge them if they can or cannot afford herbs or three visits a week. Bear in mind that patient outcomes are the most important thing, and if a lack of finances is an issue, you can always negotiate.

Greg Bantick
In practice since 1980
Health & Healing Wellness Centre (Brisbane, QLD)
www.healthhealingwellness.net.au

How do you determine success in your own clinic?

My main criteria of success are that I listen to and understand what patients want and, also, that I am successful in helping them with their particular problems. It's about being good at understanding what your patients want and expect, especially when they come in with multiple issues. It's important to know what they would like to get out of the interaction with you. I am unable to offer that without access to patients and providing them with a safe place to come to.

My ability to do that is dependent on me having a certain level of financial security and a strong business foundation as well. Success for me also is feeling safe and secure in my business and having good relationships with other colleagues and staff.

A high level of ongoing enthusiasm for clinical problem-solving and the study around it help me to feel successful. It's backing up the front end of looking after patients. For this to occur we also need goodness within our community.

When you first started out, what did you do well and what should you have done differently?

It was more by accident than choice that I found two good mentors (senior practitioners in Brisbane) during my early beginnings. I was able to work with them a few days a week. This provided me with a sense of what was required in business, patient care and staff management. It also gave me a stable income in the early days of my practice. I also assisted the first Chinese medicine school in Brisbane with academic administrating and teaching. This supplemented my income.

When I was starting out in the mid-1970s, most people we saw were people who had been let down by biomedicine as no treatment was available for them. They were difficult and complex cases with serious problems. This caused a lot of pressure for practitioners at the time, because books, resources and senior practitioners were scarce. Responding to very serious health concerns of patients at that time was demanding and tiresome. It took its toll on practitioners and left a legacy. It also left little time for acquiring business skills as we had to react to difficult situations arising in the clinic on a daily basis.

Mistakes that I made were with my clinical interaction mostly, as I wanted more from my patients than they wanted for themselves. They were not open to diet and lifestyle changes and, by jumping too far ahead, I probably lost some patients along the way.

Studying the medicine and philosophy was more interesting to me than finding out how to run a business, as I am not naturally interested in those details, however in my recent teaching positions I have now pushed for this to be included in courses.

I am not good at promoting myself and I took a long time to be comfortable in advertising and marketing myself. We need to find our own way with what we are good at and most comfortable with. In my case, instead of offering specials, I much prefer putting things out there that are educational and thus tell people who I am and what I do. Transferring knowledge that empowers people towards better self-care is my highest priority, rather than focusing on marketing that encourages dependency.

What is most important to you in your practice today?

Not too many things have changed. I really want to hear what my patients want, then diagnose their conditions in a way they understand and, finally, come up with a treatment plan with an appropriate timeline.

These days I am a lot more confident in dealing with difficult conditions, in suggesting to patients to come in once a week or once a fortnight, or in telling them they will have to take herbs for 12 to 18 months. I also feel more at ease in pointing out possible aggravating factors to patients and changes they could make that would help relieve their condition and facilitate their recovery. I can now have this conversation upfront and establish an easier and cleaner relationship.

It's still important to me to develop my skills to listen, to see, to touch and to pinpoint what it all means in our medicine. I particularly enjoy reading and expanding my skills. It frequently brings tears to my eyes when I read the Nei Jing or Shang Han Lun as I am deeply impressed by their profound insight.

It's very important to have clear boundaries as to what I can and can't do for people. By doing this, I feel less burdened having to fix patients and their problems.

I enjoy other activities outside the clinic that fill me up and are nourishing, such as ongoing study of Chinese calligraphy and drawing which I find essential for clinic work. I could still be better at advertising and marketing. We tend to do things in certain ways but it is important to be adaptable.

What do you think can be done to improve the Chinese medicine profession?

I would like to see students graduate from their courses with a feeling of great confidence in knowing what they know and being able to use it; enthusiasm for lifelong learning developed through their training; personal skills to build a rapport with people with serious illness in often difficult personal circumstances; and the ability to maintain themselves and their skills objectively in the midst of that.

I think graduates could be better prepared to be small business people as that's how we tend to operate in Australia. There are very few resources available to our profession as we cannot join a big practice or a hospital.

In clinic, we need to continue to develop our clinical skills, techniques and knowledge in prescribing herbs. We need to become better at establishing community and networks. Once a month, I still meet with colleagues who all have 40+ years' experience.

A unique element to our profession is that we are often approached by people who have tried other modalities without help or success. They are desperate. Therefore, we are often in the position of having to perform many roles in attending to a patient's problems.

What important tip would you give to a graduate just starting out?

Find more mentors; don't be afraid to ask for help. Find both a good business mentor and a clinic mentor.

> Don't be afraid to ask for help. Find both a good business mentor and a clinic mentor.

You should acknowledge and appreciate the compassionate urge to help other people that you have started to develop and respond to that.

What other advice would you give to new graduates?

It is important to keep studying at some point. You may be interested in treating particular health problems and undertake further training or study to become an expert in them.

Take care of the healer; you need to learn what it means to look after yourself so you can be your best with the work that you do.

> Look after yourself so you can be your best with the work that you do.

Jeff Shearer
In practice since 1995
Evolve Natural Medicine (Newcastle, NSW)
www.evolvenaturalmedicine.com.au

How do you determine success in your own clinic?

Success to me is a relative term and requires a mix of things. First, I need to be in love with my practice. I need to feel each day the joy that comes with assisting people to achieve better health. I have done many different jobs in my life and for me each of those became torture when I felt like it was a grind or I was simply going through the motions. So it's vital for me to feel excited and passionate about going to work. In saying that, this will not necessarily be the case every day as naturally in life we have our ups and downs. However, if I have more of the great days than not, I'm happy.

Second, I want to be able to get good results for the people who come to see me for help. So making sure I am constantly honing my skills is important even after so many years in practice. I also have to recognise that I won't always get it right and that sometimes other variables known and unknown can affect the outcome. Do your best and then let it go.

Third, for my practice to have longevity, the money coming in needs to be more than the money going out. I need to be able to make a reasonable income in order to create a long-term sustainable practice. I have to understand my practice is a business and I need to have my head around the key areas of business planning, marketing, financial management and customer service.

When you first started out, what did you do well and what should you have done differently?

I learnt early on in practice the value of communication with my clients and how to include them in their health journey. I've always been big on education and helping clients understand the power of the choices they make in their lives. So much so that I am still constantly looking at ways to improve how to educate my clients more effectively and provide them with the necessary resources that will improve their lives.

Looking back at my beginnings as a practitioner, I could have spent a lot more time learning about how to create an effective business. I spent a long time wandering around in the wasteland trying to figure out how to build a practice. I didn't like the idea of business or marketing so avoided both and suffered as a result. You see, I believed both were unethical, akin to the corporate giants who pollute our environment and have no heart. However, I have since learnt that marketing is how I can educate the community about what I do and how I can help and that my practice is a business whether I like it or not. It is how I choose to use those two things that defines my ethics and integrity. If I want to help people then this is how I do it.

What is most important to you in your practice today?

Congruence and integrity are extremely important to me. Engaging in the advice that I give my clients like dietary suggestions or regular treatments helps me to understand the struggles that they perhaps go through in addressing their own health. This helps me have empathy when they struggle. Being human I'm definitely not perfect, so recognising my humanity helps me recognise and respect theirs whilst still being able to look at better ways to help them with change.

What do you think can be done to improve the Chinese medicine profession?

It's time for us to cast aside our apathy and own our profession. As powerful as our medicine is, it is useless unless we take it more seriously and do whatever we can for the betterment of our industry and our community. We need to stand tall, be proud and advocate for our medicine, spread our message and overcome the lack of confidence we have as individuals and as a profession. It is not until we challenge our areas of discomfort that we will truly grow and take our rightful place in the health care industry. If we believe in the strength of our medicine then I believe we have a responsibility to spread the message far and wide every chance we get.

What important tip would you give to a graduate just starting out?

I always suggest when starting out to go and work for someone who is creating success in a way that resonates with you. Watch how they work, be inquisitive and investigate the nuances of what they do and why they do it. Don't just look at their point selection or their herbal prescription but how they run their business as this is where the real keys to success live. I have seen many a brilliant practitioner fail due to not understanding how to run a business properly.

What other advice would you give to new graduates?

Take your time and remember with any new journey there will be challenges along the way. If you are not fully booked in a couple of months understand that this is actually normal.

Navigating the world of practice is a huge endeavour. Be kind to yourself along the way. Enjoy the wins and learn from your mistakes as both are part of practice. And never give up, because what you do really matters.

Peter Gigante
In practice since 1989
East West Therapies (Romsey, VIC)
www.eastwesttherapies.net.au

How do you determine success in your own clinic?

Success is when I witness transformation of my patients as a result of my intervention. It's about a value proposition for both – the patient and myself. The positive merits for the patient of coming to see me: they make effort, they take risks, they invest trust and they pay money to me as a measurable result of my intervention that is successful for them. The positive merits for me: by engaging with patients I become a better practitioner and that is success to me. A result of that equation is patient retention, which is an important indicator in my clinic. As I treat children in my practice, my patients can come to see me for a long time.

When you first started out, what did you do well and what should you have done differently?

I adopted a professional identity as fully and as quickly as possible. I threw myself wholeheartedly into being a Chinese medicine practitioner.

It's best to have a clear head and a strong vision about how you want to operate. I went into a partnership prematurely and the partnership dissolved amicably after 12 months. We had different visions of practice and we hadn't given it enough thought and discussion beforehand. Despite having the same amount of passion for going into practice, some business divisions do not work out.

What is most important to you in your practice today?

Communication with patients is important. When talking with patients, I am clear about everything I do and let them know exactly what I can and can't do. I inform patients what I understand their problem to be and what my intentions are for treating it. I support patients' needs and promptly responding to their questions. Patients build trust if effective communication has been maintained consistently over a long period of time.

Transparency and accessibility are also important, even in cases where the outcome is unsure and where the best treatment might have to be developed over time. Always communicate intentions clearly and honestly; that still works best for me.

What do you think can be done to improve the Chinese medicine profession?

We could do better with developing our collective identity. What does this mean? We are a profession of many parts in this great ocean of Chinese medicine that we swim in. Develop and tap into the collective wisdom of the past and present and take this into the future. There are many different practices and modes or forms that we apply. The lack of coherency of our profession diminishes the public's ability to recognise the value of Chinese medicine and means we are less effective at presenting our value as a modality in the health care industry.

While our services are available to a good part of the population, there are still many people who are unaware of or don't have access to Chinese medicine treatment. In the public domain where scepticism and ignorance remain barriers to a thriving profession, we have not effectively asserted our legitimate place within the Australian health workforce. To do that and become stronger as a profession, we need to mature further. As a profession, we are adolescents. Ethically, we are growing as a profession with the implementation of standards of behaviour and rules of practice and by presenting a positive and appropriate interface with the public. We are still learning how to handle shopfronts, signage, posters and promotions in a mature way.

What important tip would you give to a graduate just starting out?

Find a mentor, someone to help you find yourself who has travelled the road before. There are lots of ways for mentoring and someone with more experience can give guidance in whatever way is appropriate.

What other advice would you give to new graduates?

Keep learning.

Robin Marchment
In practice since 1998
Maru Chinese Medicine (Melbourne, VIC)
www.robinmarchment.com.au

How do you determine success in your own clinic?

My definition of success has never been primarily about material achievement. It makes life comfortable but, from the beginning, I have always loved what I do and count my blessings for having chosen this profession. I get tremendous satisfaction from it and have also made a very comfortable living. That is success.

Results are important both for personal satisfaction and for professional confidence. They confirm that we are doing the right thing and looking after our patients. And doing well by our patients and achieving results also means more patients come to see us. Retention is the key, and when you do well by your patients the retention rate is high. Putting patients first can mean a variety of things, including a genuine sense of care and the ability to communicate properly. All our guidelines for labelling and informed consent, for instance, are a wonderful way to show patients how professional and conscientious we are. That not only responds to what patients need but also establishes the professional relationship while developing rapport. Apart from clinical results in our profession, communication and honesty are essential to our business. And personal satisfaction cannot be separated from material success because that shows us we have 'made it'.

When you first started out, what did you do well and what should you have done differently?

I always looked after my patients well but could have been more confident about promoting myself. I was possibly too modest when I first started out: I did not even like to call my clinic by my own name so I made up a clinic name instead.

What is most important to you in your practice today?

It hasn't changed very much. The patient is always the most important. I respond to their needs appropriately and promptly. Always. They get good after-sales service from me and I always offer to be contacted at any time for queries. I still enjoy the process of consultation and get great satisfaction from it, and I am always amazed at how much my patients know about Chinese medicine after a few visits.

What do you think can be done to improve the Chinese medicine profession?

In my experience, the tendency in modern education of treating the student as a 'client' is not always to the advantage of the student. Giving too much priority to the 'client' and profitability does not always translate into the best educational outcomes. The teaching environment has changed tremendously over the past 20 years. As a profession, we have to support the fact that undergraduate degrees are only the foundation. Greater emphasis needs to be placed on postgraduate learning via clinical experience. Undergraduates and graduates alike need to understand that theoretical learning is essential but is not the most important part – attitude and integrity are what make a good practitioner.

What important tip would you give to a graduate just starting out?

Be humble but have confidence. Be honest but reassuring. Be aware of your limitations and always be open to more learning. Confidence is important but we need to strike a nice balance between simple confidence and overconfidence. We need an abundance of humility and honesty. We need to be simple and genuine rather than pretend we are something that we are not. Put patients first, promote yourself well and, above all, be honest.

What other advice would you give to new graduates?

Confidence comes with experience and it also comes with preparation and further knowledge. It is understood that you don't know it all – you just need to acknowledge the gaps in your knowledge. If you are conscientious and diligent you can fill in the blanks.

Stephen Janz
In practice since 1987
Kenmore Centre for Health (Kenmore, QLD)
www.kenmorecentreforhealth.com.au

How do you determine success in your own clinic?

I apply two measures of success: clinical outcomes and financial growth. There is no point if you can't afford to do it. My clinic is not a charity but a business and at its core is improving people's health. I am unable to do that if I am not viable in practice.

When you first started out, what did you do well and what should you have done differently?

What I did well is to let local health professionals know that I started practice. I should have looked for opportunities to interface with community organisations to break down barriers about Chinese medicine and to put a human face to it.

What is most important to you in your practice today?

It comes back to maintaining clinical outcomes, consistently helping people to achieve their health goals, and keeping a strong business focus and a vital, dynamic approach rather than being stuck in a rut. It is also important to be part of change as well as embrace change in the clinic. Do not get bored with what you do, and continue to engage with new ideas and broaden and expand the options of how you can best help people.

What do you think can be done to improve the Chinese medicine profession?

There are multiple levels. First, we need to work out what our identity is. Are you a Chinese medicine practitioner or do you want to be a primary contact health professional? Are you someone to give a patient Tai chi for back pain or a clinically proven exercise that works? Engage with the broad information available today rather than, for example, giving patients Chinese food therapy. We are health professionals first, have broad knowledge and research available to us, and we deliver that with professionalism. Be careful with limiting yourself to just Chinese medicine.

It's about our identity and what we draw on. And this should not just be the Chinese medicine model. Acupuncture is more than the Chinese medicine model. Dry needling has happened because of practitioners ignoring the classics, which created a gap in the market and a place for trigger point or ashi acupuncture.

We do well by following the long traditions but our medicine has never been static. The Chinese medicine model talks about treating according to local conditions. What cultural group? What times? What environment? We should take the holistic model and bring it into our own practice, exactly like they do in countries like South America, Canada, China and Taiwan.

What important tip would you give to a graduate just starting out?

If possible, find an experienced practitioner to bounce ideas off. It is easy to feel unsupported and isolated. Make sure you go to professional industry seminars. Develop a network and it will support you as you grow into the profession.

What other advice would you give to new graduates?

Most graduates in Australia will be running their own small business so do not underestimate the skills required to run a small business.

Remember that good communication achieves good outcomes. Communication skills would have to be a primary focus as if they are lacking, good patient rapport fails.

Treat what the patient asks you to treat. If someone has a pain in the head, treat that. You must treat what the patient comes to see you for.

Steven Clavey
In practice since 1986
Apricot Grove (Melbourne, VIC)
www.stevenclavey.com

How do you determine success in your own clinic?

Basically, I feel I'm successful when I have enough patients to fill up the time I've got available and I'm not sitting around waiting. Also, it's a matter of making sure that the students in my clinic are being trained properly. If we are attending to enough patients so that the students can see a variety of different things and they are learning, then we are in good shape. Also, I have other practitioners at the clinic and we continue learning together all the time.

As long as everyone is interested in improving their Chinese medicine skills and, of course, the patients are feeling better, which I think has to be a given, then that's success for me.

When you first started out, what did you do well and what should you have done differently?

Because I started off in gynaecology, I started seeing patients only once a month and that's one of the big things I would have done differently. When you first begin, I think you should see patients once a week. Then, when they start to improve a little bit, you should reward them by saying, "Okay, I'll see you in two weeks now". And then as they improve more, extend that to three weeks, then four weeks and so on. In this way, you learn more quickly because your feedback comes more quickly.

In terms of starting off, start small. I began in a small room doing acupuncture and I had a very small space for herbs – maybe only 40 or 50 herbs. As I learnt those herbs, I added more and more. That's the best way because it's not very expensive to start off small and you can then base your expansion on your profit. The worst thing to do when starting out is to spend a lot of money setting up a beautiful clinic and then having to worry about paying for it.

What is most important to you in your practice today?

This comes back to the same question about success – making sure patients get results and are happy and healthy, that students are learning and that we are making enough money to provide a living for the people in our practice. As long as we're meeting those goals and we're not in the red, then everybody is happy. We should be not overworking but also not underworking either.

What do you think can be done to improve the Chinese medicine profession?

One thing that we should be doing a lot more of is sharing our successes. If you find a good way of doing something, make sure you share it with other people.

Our big thing right now is we have to make sure that the grassroots – the patients – are happy. We have to make sure that people start to see Chinese medicine as something they cannot do without, because once we are noticed by big money competition like pharmaceutical companies and so on, we're in trouble. It's sobering to remember that 100 years ago there was a homeopathic hospital here in Melbourne. So, we have to do a lot of very strong grassroots work to make sure that we have a good foundation and people see us as essential to their health. And, of course, we should be talking to doctors too so that they realise we do different things to them so are not in competition.

What important tip would you give to a graduate just starting out?

Be aware that it takes about five years to get a clinic going, so don't panic if you don't have a lot of patients in the first few months. It takes three years at least to start making a living from your clinic so that's another reason to start small and avoid any really high overheads. Start small, take your time and get in with senior practitioners who can help you out because they had to do exactly the same thing once. Work to your strengths – that's another good place to start.

Work to your strengths.

What other advice would you give to new graduates?

You are not done yet. You're not done learning. You'll never finish learning with Chinese medicine. Don't think you're done. You have to read a lot, talk to other people and get into groups where you can hone your skills. Go back and study with other people. You have just begun and only just laid the foundation, so keep going. It will be fun!

In essence...

'Never settle for mediocre outcomes' is a great statement by Clare Pyers. I absolutely love it as it reflects exactly what I do at work every day. I am always there for my patients but make it clear where the line is. Financial security is important for me, for you and for everyone else in the industry and, as many have shown us already in this Element, we can achieve it. What I have also learnt from these conversations is that we are a team of very talented individuals trying to make a difference to our patients. As we keep learning from one another, we keep building our profession and the impact of Chinese medicine, creating resilience and improving health along the way.

When speaking to my aforementioned colleagues, a few topics were consistently addressed and discussed. Here is a brief summary:

Building a clinic and business takes time

Please remember at all times that Rome wasn't built in a day. To create a successful clinic and business takes time. It takes ample time too, not just a few months. But on the other side of the coin, you are in it for the long run and you can practise, literally, until you drop. It has always been an attractive feature to me that I can practise until I am 80 or practise on the go anywhere in the world.

Lack of support for new graduates

Unfortunately, there is not enough support around for new graduates to find help in the first few years. Finding a mentor is one of the priorities highly recommended by my colleagues. They were all happy to offer their assistance and guidance in this book as they know how important mentorship is during the first few years.

Better training needed in running a business

The lack of training in establishing and running a business was also addressed by my colleagues. During undergraduate education there is not enough emphasis on business management skills, hence you must learn everything at once when you start your practice. The recommendation once again is to learn from someone else first and attend courses that teach business essentials.

Good communication skills are a must

Managing your patients is much easier with good communication skills. You will continuously educate your patients on lifestyle changes, treatment approaches, expectations on progress, the importance of maintenance sessions and the prevention of health problems. This includes knowing your boundaries (ie. what you can and can't do) and communicating them accordingly and honestly. The importance of community connection was noted by several colleagues and this aligns well with excellent communication skills.

ELEMENTAL SELF-CARE

If you don't respect yourself, how can you display respect to anyone else?

'Respect' can be defined as "a positive feeling or action shown towards someone or something considered important, or held in high esteem or regard; it conveys a sense of admiration for good or valuable qualities; and it is also the process of honouring someone by exhibiting care, concern, or consideration for their needs or feelings".[20]

I have found that there is a tendency for low self-esteem in our industry. Please remember each and every day that *you* are the most important thing in *your* life and to show respect to yourself above all else.

ELEMENT 5 ACTIVITIES

You have made it to the last Element and the last set of activities. Spend ample time with these questions and revisit them every 12 months.

5.1: Your quality management cycle

Implementing a quality management cycle in your practice is a good way to keep your finger on the pulse and keep improving what you do.

1. Plan: What area in your current business or practice needs addressing?
2. Do: Think of a change that will make that area better?
3. Check: What was achieved with this change?
4. Act: Revise and implement the change and note your learnings.
5. Have you set a rhythm or flow for your quality management system, for example, monthly, quarterly or yearly? Are there other areas or elements of your business that should be included in your PDCA cycle?

5.2: Learn from yourself and others

1. How are you learning from your mistakes?
2. Have you determined what you consider success for your business or practice?
3. From reading the practitioner interviews, what must you remember, particularly when things are tough or challenging?

Congratulations, you are a winning success now! For further worksheets and templates, go to www.brigittelinder.com.

CONCLUSION

The aim of this book is to help newly qualified Chinese medicine practitioners transition into practice and establish a rewarding long-term career and a business with a substantial disposable income. One of the key messages is to keep learning. Learn from the ones who have done it before you. Take advantage of their advice.

The Chinese medicine profession is a wonderful legacy of a system surviving centuries, civilisations, wars, and the crises and brutalities of the world. It takes a special interest, a deep connection to ancient wisdom and a dose of tradition to embrace it and apply it in a 21st-century setting.

Be aware of the path ahead and plan for it accordingly. This is one of the most important things in your business journey. Be clear on the implications of your plan. Find support if you are not able to move forward or solve a problem. Put energy and time into finding a mentor, building a supportive network and creating a system for regular reviews with colleagues. Remain connected and active with your alumni groups; it will pay off. Do not let yourself slide into isolation.

Also vital is focusing on your business skills. If you know that you are not well versed in conducting business-oriented tasks, either seek a position where you don't have to worry about it or get help and employ people who can do it for you. The key is to know what you can and cannot do. Remain connected to the goal of improving your business skills.

Keep establishing bridges to help yourself become excellent in what you do both as a practitioner and a human being. Help fellow practitioners in their business journey too. In doing this, you become a role model for the next generation and help them find better access to the profession.

Organisation is a part of running both a clinic and a business; the more streamlined you are in your work, the more effective and consistent you become. Never forget that excellence is the standard to aim for. If you are overtaken by complacency or laziness, recognise it and get assistance to find your way back onto the path.

Lastly, show gratitude for everything that happens in your life.

I hope you enjoyed reading this book and find it a valuable resource during your business journey.

I would love your feedback on how you are going. Please take a few minutes to complete the short survey online at:

www.brigittelinder.com

APPENDIX 1

RESOURCES AND HELP

This section provides a summary of recommended organisations that can provide support and assist with various issues. It also lists industry partners and suppliers. The only organisation that has financially contributed to this book is Conforma N.V. (Belgium) who supply liquid extracts, have a GMP licence and are cleared by the TGA.

RECOMMENDED ORGANISATIONS

Mentoring

- **Chinese Medicine Health Alliance (CMHA)**

  CMHA provides details of mentors and coaches offering postgraduate support.

  www.chinesemedicinehealthalliance.com.au

- **Australian Acupuncture and Chinese Medicine Association (AACMA)**

  AACMA offers its members a 24month mentoring program connecting experienced practitioners with students in their final year of study or within two years of graduation. Online registration is available for both mentees and mentors.

  www.acupuncture.org.au/mentoring-program

Coaching

- **Ethical Practice**

  Ethical Practice offer individual and workplace coaching. They also run live and online seminars. Free resources for both new and established practitioners are available on their website.

  www.ethicalpractice.net

Online seminars

- **Lotus Institute of Integrative Medicine** | www.elotus.org
- **ProD Seminars** | www.prodseminars.net
- **Ethical Practice** | www.ethicalpractice.net

Live seminars

- **China Books (Melbourne and Sydney)** | www.chinabooks.com.au
- **Ethical Practice** | www.ethicalpractice.net

Podcasts

- **Heavenly Qi** | www.heavenlyqipodcast.com
- **Yin Yang Podcast** | www.yinyangpodcast.com
- **Chinese Medicine Central** | www.chinesemedicinecentral.com
- **Everyday Acupuncture Podcast** | www.everydayacupuncturepodcast.com
- **PinPoint Performance** | www.pinpointperformance.training
- **Acupuncturist on Fire** | https://itunes.apple.com/us/podcast/acupuncturist-on-fire/id1001203922?mt=2

Australian regulatory agency for therapeutic goods

- **Therapeutic Goods Administration (TGA)** | www.tga.gov.au

Regulatory agencies for the Chinese medicine profession

- **Australian Health Practitioner Regulation Agency (AHPRA)** | www.ahpra.gov.au

- **Chinese Medicine Board of Australia (CMBA)** | www. chinesemedicineboard.gov.au

Chinese medicine professional associations in Australia

- **Australian Acupuncture and Chinese Medicine Association (AACMA)** | www.acupuncture.org.au

- **Federation of Chinese Medicine & Acupuncture Societies of Australia Ltd (FCMA)** | **www.fcma.org.au**

- **Chinese Medicine & Acupuncture Society of Australia (CMASA)** | **www.australiantcm.com.au/cmasaNew/index. php**

- **Traditional Medicine of China Society (Australia) (TMCSA)** | **www.tmcsa.stcm.com.au**

- **Chinese Medicine Industry Council of Australia Ltd (CMIC)** | **www.cmic-aus.org.au**

- **Australian Traditional-Medicine Society (ATMS)** | www. atms.com.au

- **Australian Natural Therapists Association (ANTA)** | www. australiannaturaltherapistsassociation.com.au

Chinese medicine practitioner action group

- **Chinese Medicine Health Alliance Australia (CMHAA)** | **www.chinesemedicinehealthalliance.com.au**

CHINESE MEDICINE CLINIC SUPPLIERS

Many of the following suppliers of needles, herbs, books and clinic materials offer a discount to students and new graduates. Please contact suppliers directly for information.

NOTE: The information in the table below is current at the time of publication.

Supplier name	Benefits	Contact details
Acuneeds Australia	• Representatives are Chinese medicine practitioners and are happy to provide assistance and support for graduates. • Fixed 15% discount to student practitioners which is extended for a newly graduated practitioner's first clinic set-up order.	www.acuneeds.com
Acupuncture Australia	• Range of practitioner products.	www.acupa.com.au
Chang Hong Trading Pty Ltd	• Range of raw herbs.	www. chineseherbswholesaler. com.au
Chinawest Pty Ltd	• Distribute hospital-grade single herb granules from China.	www.chinawest.com.au
China Books Melbourne	• Range of practitioner products including books. • Organise live seminars and workshops for practitioners. • New graduates in the first year of practice receive 5–10% discount on needles, herbs and clinic products. • Student rates apply for workshops and seminars.	www.chinabooks.com.au

China Books Sydney	• Range of practitioner products including books. • Organise live seminars and workshops for practitioners.	Ph: 02 9280 1885
Empirical Health	• Claim to supply the highest quality of raw herbs in Australia.	www.empiricalhealthshop.com.au
Helio Supply Co	• Range of practitioner products. • No delivery fee for the first order. • Provide samples of acupuncture needles.	www.heliosupply.com.au
Materia Medica Limited (New Zealand)	• Subsidiary of Yes Chinaherb. • Supply Koda herbal extract range.	www.kodaherbs.com
NeedlePro Australia	• DongBang acupuncture needle range. • Provide health practice success seminars.	www.needlepro.com.au
San Acupuncture Supplies & Equipment	• Range of practitioner products. • Pride themselves of outstanding customer service.	www.sanacupuncturesupplies.com.au
Sun Herbal	• Herbal products such as ChinaMed® capsules and Black Pearl® pills.	www.sunherbal.com
Wellspring Bookstore	• Variety of books on Chinese medicine and other complementary therapies.	www.endeavourbookstore.com.au
Winner Trading Pty Ltd	• Herbal products for practitioners including the Eurofins certified range.	www.chineseherbsonline.com.au
Yes Chinaherb Pty Ltd	• Herbal products for practitioners.	www.yeschinaherb.com

APPENDIX 2

RECOMMENDED READING

Business practices

Abundance: The Future Is Better Than You Think
Peter H. Diamandis & Steven Kotler
ISBN-13: 978-1451614213

Focus: The Hidden Driver of Excellence
Daniel Goleman
ISBN-13: 978-0062114969

Goals! How to Get Everything You Want – Faster Than You Ever Thought Possible
Brian Tracy
ISBN-13: 978-1605094113

Making Acupuncture Pay: Real-World Advice for Successful Private Practice
Matthew D. Bauer
ISBN-13: 978-1457502798

Personal Kanban: Mapping Work | Navigating Life
Jim Benson & Tonianne DeMaria Barry
ISBN-13: 978-1453802267

Points for Profit: The Essential Guide to Practice Success for Acupuncturists
Honora Lee Wolfe, Eric Strand & Marilyn Allen
ISBN-13: 978-1891845253

The 7 Habits of Highly Effective People
Stephen R. Covey
ISBN-13: 978-1471129391

The Power of Full Engagement
Jim Loehr & Tony Schwartz
ISBN-13: 978-0743226752

Traction: Get a Grip on Your Business
Gino Wickman
ISBN-13: 978-1936661831

Chinese medicine skills and patient rapport

Five Element Constitutional Acupuncture
Angela Hicks, John Hicks & Peter Mole
ISBN-13: 978-0702031755

Understanding the Difficult Patient: A Guide for Practitioners of Oriental Medicine
Nancy Bilello
ISBN-13: 978-1891845321

APPENDIX 3

REFERENCES

1. PayScale. Research [Internet]. Seattle WA: PayScale; 2018 [cited 2019 January 13]. Available from: www.payscale.com/research/AU/Skill=Acupuncture/Salary

2. MindTools. What are your values? [Internet]. Swindon: Mind Tools; 2018 [cited 2018 July 15]. Available from: www.mindtools.com/pages/article/newTED_85.htm

3. Tracy B. Goals! How to Get Everything You Want – Faster Than You Ever Thought Possible. San Francisco: Berrett-Koehler Publishers, 2010;13.

4. McDonald J, Janz S. The Acupuncture Evidence Project: A Comparative Literature Review (Revised Edition). Brisbane: Australian Acupuncture and Chinese Medicine Association Ltd, 2017. Available from: www.acupuncture.org.au/resources/publications/the-acupuncture-evidence-project-a-comparative-literature-review-2017

5. Stuyt EB, Voyles CA. The National Acupuncture Detoxification Association protocol, auricular acupuncture to support patients with substance abuse and behavioral health disorders: current perspectives. Subst Abuse Rehabil. 2016;7:169-180. Available from: www.ncbi.nlm.nih.gov/pmc/articles/PMC5153313

6. Hullender Rubin LE, Anderson BJ, Craig LB. Acupuncture and *in vitro* fertilisation research: current and future directions. Acupunct Med. 2018;36:117-122. Available from: https://aim.bmj.com/content/36/2/117

7. Cancer Research UK. Turmeric [Internet]. London: Cancer Research UK; 2018 [cited 2018 February 18]. Available from: www.cancerresearchuk.org/about-cancer/cancer-in-general/treatment/complementary-alternative-therapies/individual-therapies/turmeric

8. Fung FY, Linn YC. Developing traditional Chinese medicine in the era of evidence-based medicine: current evidences and challenges. Evid Based Complement Alternat Med. 2015;2015:425037. Available from: www.hindawi.com/journals/ecam/2015/425037

9. World Health Organization. Ensuring Good Dispensing Practices. (MDS-3: Managing Access to Medicines and Health Technologies). Geneva: WHO Essential Medicines and Health Products Information Portal, 2012;30. Available from: http://apps.who.int/medicinedocs/en/d/Js19607en

10. Department of Industry, Innovation and Science. Unfair contracts and sham contracts [Internet]. Australian Government business.gov.au; [cited 2018 April 20]. Available from: www.business.gov.au/people/contractors/independent-contractors/unfair-contracts-and-sham-contracts

11. Moore A, Canaway R, O'Brien KA. Chinese medicine students' preparedness for clinical practice: an Australian survey. J Alternative Complementary Medicine, 2010;16(7).

12. Fair Work Commission. Health Professionals and Support Services Award 2010 [MA000027] [Internet]. ACT: Fair Work Commission, 2010 [updated 2018 Nov 11; cited 2018 December 8]. Available from: www.fwc.gov.au/documents/documents/modern_awards/award/ma000027/default.htm

13. Marano, H. Why most small businesses fail within the first three years. 2018 Jan 23. In: https://insidesmallbusiness.com.au [Internet]. Sydney: Octomedia. 2018. Available from: https://insidesmallbusiness.com.au/planning-management/why-most-small-businesses-fail-within-the-first-three-years

14. Benson J, DeMaria Barry T. Personal Kanban: Mapping Work | Navigating Life. Scotts Valley: CreateSpace Independent Publishing Platform, 2011.

15. Bowen, JL. How accountability leads to success. Jan L. Bowen; 2015 Dec 15. [cited 2017 December 24]. Available from: https://janlbowen.com/how-accountability-leads-to-success

16. HealthTimes. Practice management software comparison. St Kilda: HealthTimes. [updated 2016 June 17; cited 2018 February 25]. Available from: https://healthtimes.com.au/hub/healthcare-it/29/guidance/nc1/practice-management-software-comparison/1691/

17. MindTools. Active listening: hear what people are really saying. [Internet]. Swindon: MindTools; 2018 [cited 2018 February 26]. Available from: www.mindtools.com/CommSkll/ActiveListening.htm

18. Worsley Institute. Worsley Five-Element Acupuncture [Internet]. Portland, OR: Worsley Institute; 2015 [cited 2018 June 9]. Available from: https://worsleyinstitute.com/worsley-five-element-acupuncture

19. MindTools. Plan-Do-Check-Act (PDCA): Continually Improving, in a Methodical Way. [Internet]. Swindon: MindTools; 2016 [cited 2018 July 7]. Available from: www.mindtools.com/pages/article/newPPM_89.htm

20. Wikipedia contributors. Respect. [Internet]. Wikipedia, The Free Encyclopedia. [updated 2018 November 26; cited 2018 December 13]. Available from: https://en.wikipedia.org/wiki/Respect

ABOUT THE
AUTHOR

Brigitte Linder practises in Australia and is registered in the divisions of Acupuncture, Chinese herbal medicine and Chinese herbal medicine dispensing. She owns and directs Safflower, a herbal dispensary and acupuncture clinic where she is the senior practitioner.

Brigitte is a self-confessed advocate for quality, change and progress in the Chinese medicine profession. She has been in the industry for 17 years and understands the difficulty in finding both a style and a framework that is compelling and successful. Brigitte is particularly active in assisting new graduates find their own rhythm and style, so they can run a successful clinic that provides them with a good income and personal satisfaction.

"I find that around 70% of new graduates feel out of their depth when entering the Chinese medicine profession," says Brigitte. She notes that among new graduates there is a lack of planning and goal setting, and a lack of confidence in achieving a sustainable income, especially in the first two to three years of practice. That's where Brigitte wishes to step in and empower and guide new practitioners.

Brigitte loves connecting with people of various backgrounds to learn from them – with this rich and cumulative knowledge, she feels there is great potential to create a thriving industry. She is a big fan of collaboration across fields and paradigms.

A dedicated practitioner, Brigitte is devoted to the integration of the rich ancient traditions of Chinese medicine into 21st-century expectations. She is constantly looking for more optimal ways to practise and teach Chinese medicine and is interested in finding ways to overcome hurdles that stop the industry from thriving.

To connect with Brigitte, please visit www.brigittelinder.com.

CONTINUE THE CONVERSATION

Thank you for sharing my passion for the Chinese medicine industry.

If you have any feedback in relation to this book or ideas for improvement in our profession, please get in touch via email at welcome@brigittelinder.com.

For additional resources and contact information, you can visit my website at www.brigittelinder.com.

You can also follow my social media channels:

Instagram: tcmgirl
Twitter: briglind
Facebook: Brigitte Linder

To reinforce and implement the content you have studied in this book, please consider joining my group mentorship program. This mentorship program facilitates essential connection with other members of the profession. Please visit my website for full details and to register.

If you are a new graduate or a seasoned practitioner who spends too much time dispensing herbs or maintaining a dispensary, please contact my dispensary, Safflower Chinese Medicine Dispensary, via www.safflower.com.au to explore how we can help you in your day-to-day practice.

www.ingramcontent.com/pod-product-compliance
Lightning Source LLC
Chambersburg PA
CBHW060040030426
42334CB00019B/2412